# The
# Marriage
# Makers

## Paul D. Freed

Insight Publishing

Insight Publishing
Box 70, Orlando, FL 32802

Scripture taken from the NEW AMERICAN STANDARD BIBLE, © The Lockman Foundation 1960, 1962, 1963, 1968, 1971, 1972, 1973, 1975, 1977, 1995. Used by permission.

---

Library of Congress Cataloging-in-Publication Data

Freed, Paul D.
    The Marriage Makers / Paul D. Freed.
    ISBN 0-9677293-0-0
        1. Marriage. 2. Family. I. Freed, Paul D.   II. Title.
    301.42                                         00-090380

---

Printed in the United States of America

05   04   03   02   01
5    4    3    2    1

# Dedication

To Sandy, my lover and my friend

# Contents

# Introduction

We received a coupon in the mail recently, for one of those oil change specials. I thought, "That's not a bad deal." It included the filter and complete oil change. We took the car down to the shop. Now, we hadn't tried this garage before, but we left the car there for an hour. When we came back, we paid them and headed on down the road. After about an hour and a half we saw a little bit of smoke coming out of the front of the car. I thought, "I wonder what that is; they must have spilled some oil or something." I wasn't paying much attention, deciding to keep driving and went down the road another 15 or 20 minutes. Suddenly we heard, "Boom!" and this awful black smoke began pouring out of the car as it shook violently. We pulled it off to the side of the road and realized that we were not going anywhere. We had the car towed back to the shop where we had the oil change done. After a few hours we found out they had drained the oil out, given us a brand new oil filter, charged us and sent us down the road, but had left out a little detail. They had forgotten to put oil back in the vehicle. Evidently, cars work better with oil, because it took a $3,000 engine job and about three months before we were finally driving our car again. We got all this for only the coupon special!

I don't know what you did with your marriage certificate, whether you put it in a drawer or tacked it up on the wall. Nevertheless, we keep going down the road of life. We start having kids and jobs and houses and all the things that we do, and forget to put some fresh "oil" back into our marriage. The best marriage needs it (at least every 3,000 "miles"). We all need some good input for our homes. Someone said to me recently, "I don't need marriage input, we have a good marriage." That is like saying "I had a great meal last month!" I don't know about you, but I like to eat three meals a day. We will invest in many things but so often we will just let our marriages hang out there. We let them stagnate and do the best they can.

Just over a generation ago in this nation, there were nine divorces out of every 1,000 marriages[1]. It is no longer nine out of 1,000. It is now 492 divorces for every 1,000 marriages. We are looking right at the implosion of the home in a cataclysmic social event that is unprecedented in this nation's history. It has happened in one generation! In fact, nearly every person in our culture has been impacted by the "divorce culture." We have seen marriage collapsing all around us.

I was recently out having dinner with my wife after one of our conferences and I was still wearing a name tag that said "Marriage Makers." The waiter came up, looked at my name tag and said, "Marriage Makers, what in the world is that?" I told him, "We do marriage conferences all around the country. We want to strengthen homes and marriages." Do you know what he said? He looked right at us and defiantly said, "Everyone I know is either divorced or getting divorced." Everyone he knows! Then he asked a question. When he said it, it gave me chills; it still affects me just thinking that he actually spoke it. He said, "Isn't marriage over?" How staggering! We have now come to the place in our culture and our society where people are actually asking the question, isn't the institution of marriage passé, isn't it finished, isn't it over? We rightly shake our heads "no." But, why is the answer "no"? The answer is "no" because **God created marriage;** not because of what we do with it, whether we succeed or fail. The point is, God is the one who started the marital union; it was His idea! In fact, the first human relationship was a marriage. Who performed the first wedding? **God did.** When God brought the first two people together, He started with a **marriage**.

> The first human relationship was a marriage.

He could have started anywhere. God could have started with a whole nation, but He didn't. He started with the home and with a marriage.

The *Song of Solomon* reveals to us God's heart for marriage. Solomon, the author of the *Song of Solomon*, reigned between 971 BC and 931 BC. He wrote the book early in his reign, around 960 – 958 BC. This is very important, because at this point in history he was married to one wife, only **one.** He was married to the Shulammite from a little village named Shulam in southern Lebanon. Solomon wrote 1,000 songs and 3,000 proverbs. But, right in the middle of our

Bible, we find a whole book devoted to love, lovemaking and the marital relationship.

This fantastic little book has insights and keys that have become nearly forgotten in our culture.

> The wisdom of God can still energize and lead our lives to new heights.

However, as always, the wisdom of God can still energize and lead our lives to new heights.

# Chapter 1

# Brides Are
# First Women

Our first Marriage Maxim is

## Brides are first women.

We men say, "Isn't that obvious!" However, subconsciously we often look for our wives to think and act like us. We want them to root for the same football team we root for, fish in the same fishing holes we like to fish at, and even use the same lures. Subconsciously we so often think that our wife should be liking the same things we do. But in fact, they're different. They're really different! Before they were ever our brides, they were **women**. "Brides are first women."

## A Woman's Greatest Needs

Song of Solomon 1:2-4a 'May he kiss me with the kisses of his mouth! For your love is better than wine. ³Your oils have a pleasing fragrance, your name is *like* purified oil; . . . ⁴Draw me after you and let us run *together!*

The Shulammite (Solomon's wife) is starting right off, stating a woman's five greatest needs. They are **affection**, **expression**, **communion**, **attraction** and **union**.

## *Affection*

First, **affection**. She is saying there in verse 2, '**May he kiss me.**' Now when I was at Oxford University in England, I got an opportunity to study from the John Wycliffe, the first English Bible, Manuscript 369. Just my professor and I were locked in a room for two weeks with the 1382 Wycliffe Manuscript. As I had a chance to study it, the first words in *Song of Solomon* were '**Kiss he me.**' No wonder most of our preachers don't use this Sunday mornings. It is a very intimate book. But when you talk about marriage and the intimacy of marriage, it opens right up. So here the Shulammite is stating, '**May he kiss me.**' A woman's first greatest need is for **affection**, gentleness, care, sensitivity and tenderness.

## *Expression*

The second greatest need of a woman is **expression**. It says in the second verse, '**Your love is better than wine.**' So expression is to be told that you are loved, cared about and special. How important it is for us men to tell our wives that we care about her, for her to hear our appreciation of her from her looks and attractiveness to her efforts in the home and marriage. Not assuming "that's her job," "her responsibility," but rather expressing our interest, loyalty and

> The small, little energies she spends, to have them noticed, gets lots of investment.

gratitude for the small and large things she does. The small, little energies she spends, to have them noticed, gets lots of investment in the marriage and, if not undercut by anger, jealousy and unforgiveness, then lots of return.

## Communion

The third greatest need of a woman is **communion**. It says there in verse 3, *'Your name is like purified oil.'* That is oil that has been filtered and has come through the process of purification. Communion is a woman's need for communication. In the *Song of Solomon* there are eight lines by the brothers, nineteen lines by the daughters of Jerusalem and twenty-seven lines by the poet or narrator. How about the king? You guessed it. He's king. There are one hundred twenty-one lines by King Solomon. That is a lot of talking, until you look at the Shulammite. She did not have one hundred twenty-one lines. She had **two** hundred twenty-one lines. In fact, this lady had more to say in the *Song of Solomon* than everybody else put together!

We say, "Ah, just a yacky lady." Umm, not so fast now. Modern research has shown that the average man speaks twelve thousand words in an average day. The average woman speaks twenty-five thousand words! In fact, if you do the ratio of what was in the *Song of Solomon* and what modern research has shown, guess what, they are **identical**.

How critical it is that our communication be two way in a marriage. "Filtered," back and forth. That we are really hearing each other, really listening. Taking the perspective of our spouse. Really trying to understand her pressures, trials, hopes and dreams.

To commune is more than just physically being together. It's a heart touch, a feeling your mate's feelings. The callousness of assuming on our spouse, not really caring to make the effort to "find" her, is a real marital freeze.

## *Attraction*

Number four is **attraction**. It says in verse four, **'Draw me after you.'** You know, we're different, really, really different. Are you aware how different we are? In every drop of male blood, there are a thousand more red blood cells than in a drop of female blood. A woman's body has 20% muscle weight; a man's has 40% muscle weight. There are one and a half gallons of blood in every male body on average and three quarters of a gallon of blood in every female body. Women have thinner skin. Men have thicker skulls. Ladies say, "I didn't need to read this book to figure that one out!" But really we're different emotionally, different psychologically; obviously we're different biologically and physiologically. In eighth grade science class, we were taught that opposites attract. Marriage should bring attraction, opposite drawn to opposite. So often we do not understand how to handle our differences and they end up making tension. If we really understand our differences and are willing to work with our differences, they should and will bring us together.

## Union

Number five is **union**, being one. It says in verse four, **'let us run *together.'*** God means for us to be one. It's as if two great war horses were running together and encouraging each other. Though they are different, they steady each other and lead each other onward in the great journey of life. Union: to be one, united in purpose concerning the children (though our methods may be different). United in direction in our faith (though time spent in devotions or the way we pray may be quite different). United in motivation with in-laws, finances and romance (though how we view them may be uniquely different).

---

**A Woman's Greatest Needs**
Affection
   Expression
      Communion
         Attraction
            Union

---

Song of Solomon 1:4b, '**We will rejoice in you and be glad; we will extol your love more than wine.**'

Here these Daughters of Jerusalem or these friends of the bride are rejoicing in her marriage. You want to have friends that are **supporting** your marriage. You do not want to have friends that are tearing your husband down. You do not want to have friends that are ripping your wife up. You want to gather friends around you that are building marriage and building up your mate. Supportive friends are so important in marriage.

> gather friends around you that are building marriage

## Expressions of Love

I would like to give the men a few "Expressions of Love." Here are six different ways you can express your love for your wife.

### MATERIAL LOVE

Number one is obvious: **Material Love**. This is the Valentine's stuff: candles, flowers, perfume, all those little "love you's." You want to express your love to your spouse **life long** through material things. When you were dating, you started giving each other things. There were those little gifts. But you do not want to let that end in your marriage; you want to keep that going.

We were at a conference about two years ago. Afterwards, a lady wrote to us, and there was a ribbon there in the letter. The letter said, "This is a ribbon off a single flower my husband got me after the conference. I took **hope** from that one flower." Something so simple can be a joy. Material Love.

## VERBAL LOVE

Number two: **Verbal Love**. This means we actually tell our wife that she is special, we care about her, we love her. You heard about the guy that said, "I told my wife I loved her on wedding day. If anything changes, I'll let her know." We need to tell our wife that we love her and tell her **often**. We received another letter from a wife who wrote, "After the conference, my husband now tells me at least once a day that I'm 'special' or he 'cares about me' or he 'loves me.' It saved our marriage!" Can you imagine that something that simple saved their marriage? Let's practice guys: into your wife's heart give her that **Verbal Love**.

## LISTENING LOVE

Number three is **Listening Love**. This means we listen and we love her by giving her our attention. We listen **without** having the answers. That's hard for us guys. We're so utilitarian. We might think, "All right, I don't mind listening. Ready, go, I'm listening. You done? You done?" Then we retort, "Here's what you need to do. You need to do this and this," and then we're out of there. But instead, give her **listening love** without coming right back with the answers. Just give her a place to be heard. You do not want some other guy whispering, "I'll give you an ear." **You** be the one that gives her **Listening Love**.

## *LOYAL LOVE*

Number four is **Loyal Love**. This means we give a message to our wife that we are loyal to her first, loyal to her before the kids and before our job. We give her first place. We are loyal to her above everything. We can give this message to her in so many ways, with time, finances and effort.

Loyalty is more than just saying you're loyal. It is **showing** her loyalty by time spent, effort put forth, energy expended. Nothing is wrong with watching that favorite football team, but every NFL and college top 20 is not your favorite. Take the effort to be loyal to her life, interests and needs. **Loyal Love**.

## *SACRIFICIAL LOVE*

Number five is **Sacrificial Love**. This means that we are actually giving to the marriage, really giving from down deep. I watch men and I wonder what we are holding back for, wife number five, wife number six, number seven? At what point do we say, "I'm going to go ahead and make this marriage happen. I'm really going to give of myself into **this** relationship." I would guess there is something your wife has been asking you to get to around the house. Most guys smile. Maybe she has been trying to get you to do this thing for a week or even a month. Maybe it has been going on into a year and a half now. She has been asking you and you have been putting it off. Take note, **sacrificial love**.

## FRIENDSHIP LOVE

Number six is **Friendship Love**. You might as well be friends. God put the first couple in Eden to be friends, best friends. Of course what were their options, the local elephant or giraffe? He put **just two** of them in that Garden. He could have put a crowd or started with a whole family. But He placed just two of them there. I think God means for us to be friends and to work on our friendship love with one another, taking time to do what the other enjoys, supporting careers, hobbies, friendships, interests. How involved? As deeply as would truly bless your spouse.

---

**Expressions of Love**

Material Love
Verbal Love
Listening Love
Loyal Love
Sacrificial Love
Friendship Love

---

Song of Solomon 1:5 **'1 am . . . like the tents of Kedar, like the curtains of Solomon.'**

She is saying quite a bit here. The Shulammite, Solomon's wife, is comparing herself to two things. She is comparing herself to the **'tents of Kedar'** and also comparing herself to the **'curtains of Solomon.'** Let me describe the tents of Kedar. My grandfather was a missionary in Dera'a, Syria, and later a pastor in Jerusalem, so he was always going out to the Bedouin tents. He would talk about these nomadic Bedouin tribes and describe how nice and cool their tents were in the summertime sunshine. When I'm saying "nice and cool" I'm talking about 95°, because it's 120°–140° out in the blazing sun. However, they would be pleasant and warm at night, 50°–55°. In the desert, it can get cold at night. Many people are not aware of this. A desert can get really cold, down to the low 40°'s, even high 30°'s. There is nothing to block the wind. But in the tents of Kedar it's toasty and warm, much better than outside. So the Shulammite is comparing herself to the tents of Kedar, and what is being said? She is relating that she gives to the marriage and into the family the practical things of care, warmth and protection for the family. But it doesn't stop there, because she also compares herself to the curtains of Solomon made of white bisus fabric with purple. The exquisite threading of these curtains was of 20–22 karat gold. So they would literally glisten in the sunlight. The woman brings in all the beauty, sensitivity, intuition and glory into the marriage. It is the full gamut of womanhood that the Shulammite is talking about.

## Bring to Your Bride

### LEADERSHIP

You want to bring leadership to your bride. **Leadership**. I think most women don't mind being lead, but always off the cliff? Who wants to always go crashing? Bring wise leadership. This means we are the first to say those difficult words, "I'm sorry." Saying that is hard for us. Many guys will say, "Well I'll say I'm sorry as soon as she says she's sorry." Now what have you done? Subtly you have passed the leadership over to her. You say, "as soon as she says she is sorry, I'll line up and follow." But here we are saying, you be the first to say **you** are sorry. How about these words: "I forgive you" or "Forgive me." Bring leadership to your wife.

### PROTECTION

Number two: bring **protection** to your wife. There are so many things coming in against marriage. I am becoming increasingly convinced that this culture is not neutral when it comes to marriage. It is not building up the home or marriage. It's tearing them down. We as men need to provide protection for our wives and for our families.

Let me take you back in time. The year was 1555; it was a cold October morning. They brought Young Ridley and Latimer out that morning in Oxford Square.[2] On that particular morning these two men had been brought out to die. They were to be executed for the terrible crime of publicly talking about Christ! They were going to be executed by being burned at the stake, a very painful,

> "Play the man!"

hideous way to die. Young Ridley was shaking all over, and I would have been too. He was trembling while the older Latimer looked over at the younger man beside him and said just three words. He said to him, "Play the man!" In other words, **be a man**. He was of course quoting Polycarp, who in the second century had said the same thing to his disciples right before he was also burned at the stake. I want to say the same thing, let's "play the man." I see so many men cutting and running, so many guys are just blasé about their marriage: "Big deal, I can always find another wife." So many pressures are coming in, whether they are finances or in-laws or sexual temptations. So many issues are coming at the family. Let's be men. If we don't do it, who is going to do it? "Play the man" in a society that has lost its way; bring protection.

### APPROVAL

Number three: bring **approval** to your wife. This means we give a message to our wife that we approve of her. We approve of how she looks. We approve of her mind and we approve of how she treats the children. Did I say agree? No, we don't always agree with what she does, but we are giving a message to her that we approve of her; we approve of her **womanhood**. It is very important that she receive that message from us, her husband — approval.

Approval is so much more than just saying, "You look nice." It is deeply believing in her, being after her best, securing her by the knowledge you are there for her and know she will make it, she will accomplish her goals or certainly give it her best shot. The stability and strengthening that approval gives are hard to calculate. When you see a woman that is moving in quiet strength, you had better believe she has received approval from somewhere. May it be from her man!

## *HONOR*

Number four: bring **honor** to her. This means that we give a message that our wife is important to us. You know, it's upsetting when a guy is at work and you hear something like this, "Here comes the old lady." That dishonors her. Everybody laughs in the office and she is humiliated. I want to say, "I guess you're really wanting to tear your wife down. Now you must have some really bad taste because she's **your** wife." This goes into the home too. When you see the kids dishonoring Mom, where do you look? You usually look at the husband, because, if he is bringing

*The Marriage Makers*

dishonor in the home, the kids are going to pick right up on it and dishonor her as well. Bring honor to your wife.

---

**Bring to Your Bride**

Leadership
Protection
Approval
Honor

---

We were in northern Morocco, a strongly Islamic fundamentalist country. We saw a man just walking along having a good old time with not a care in the world. I guess he was numero uno, big man on campus, because he was just strutting and waving at his buddies. Directly behind him was his wife. She was carrying two huge suitcases, and he wasn't paying her a bit of attention. I felt bad for her, but not as bad as I felt for the wife behind her, or the wife behind her. This guy had **seven** wives lined up in a row. (It's a pecking order, by the way.) When you got to the poor little thing at the end, she was in big trouble. She was carrying a huge burden on her back and all these suitcases, while the other wives were kicking her back.

Every one of these wives, from wife number one to wife number seven, had something in common. They were all veiled. From their eyes were pouring two emotions: fear and bitterness.

Marriage is not meant to be drudgery. It is not to be full of bitterness, full of fear. It is meant to be a place of release, friendship, honor and joy.

## Marital Parenting Principles

We hear so much about raising kids God's way. That's good, but I'm going to come from a little different angle. I want to give you ten parenting principles that will strengthen your marriage while you are parenting. If you are just parenting for the kids, it isn't healthy. If the whole family life is for the kids, they will begin to be selfish and egocentric. So you want to parent with principles that are also building your marriage.

Number One: **Don't correct each other in front of the kids.** This does not mean that you don't have open dialog with each other privately. In front of the children, don't correct each other.

Number Two: **Remember you are the balance for them** (both of you). Usually in every marriage, one parent is a little too easy and lets them get away with too much. The other parent is coming down a little too tough. The two of you together are their balance. They need both of you. You are their balance between the **two** of you.

Number Three: **Present a singular front to the children**. For example, one parent thinks the children should be in by 9:00 p.m., and the other one thinks it should be midnight. You want to come to them with a singular front. So you say, "Be in by 10:30 tonight." You want to come to a decision in private. Don't let the kids know which one of you feels which way. What will they do if the find out? They will go to the one they can manipulate the most, so you want to present a singular front, whatever you feel in private.

Number Four: **Don't be your child's favorite**. Isn't this a temptation? You want to be your child's favorite. "Your dad or your mom doesn't understand you like I do. I really can understand you." Be careful with that. Resist that temptation to be your child's favorite. Have the **marriage** be their favorite. We're Marriage Makers!

Number Five: **Don't have a favorite child**. As much as possible, show equity with all children. If you have more than one child, invariably you are going to feel a little closer to one. This can happen if one is a little more like you or you can identify a little more with one. Be careful that you don't do that. Don't have a favorite. As much as possible, show equity with all children. This is particularly true if you have a handicapped child. The temptation is to give them extra attention to compensate for their deficiency. However, each child needs your love, care and attention. Having no resentments and no competition is the goal. No favorite is the answer.

Number Six: **Include the children in fight resolutions**. Did I say include the children in the fight? No! They already probably know there is tension. You do not have to get into all the details of what is going on between the two of you. But when you resolve it, you want the children to feel relieved. Tell them, "Mommy and Daddy worked it out. It's going to be all right." "We're not quitters." If we can get that message to them, they will learn that they are **not quitters** when it comes to gym class, their relationship with their friends, or when it comes to life. "We're not quitters." We want to get that message to our kids. So include the children in fight resolutions. We're going to work this out.

Number Seven: **In all discipline, the motivation is restoration, not punishment**. Keep in mind when you discipline them, whatever the discipline is, that your motive is to restore, not to punish. When God disciplines you, you feel like He is always trying to pull you back to Himself. So should our motivation be with our kids. We need to keep that clearly in mind. We're not disciplining them just to discipline them.

Be careful as well to not bring up forgiven mistakes. If you forgive, then do, not reminding them of past faults. Revisited issues after forgiveness is given sends a message that forgiveness didn't really happen. So remember, we're disciplining them for **restoration**.

Number Eight: **Never be hesitant to say "I'm sorry" or "I was wrong."** It doesn't diminish authority; it enhances it. Why? Because if you can say you're sorry, or you're wrong, it gives the kids a model for when they are wrong. It puts the responsibility on them that they need to be saying "I was wrong" and "I'm sorry" also. Your authority will be enhanced by being willing to admit when you are wrong.

Number Nine: **Do not believe your child is without fault.** "Oh, not my sweet little Susie. She would never do that." "Not my Johnny." Why do we think that way? Because they reflect on us. Admitting that they could actually be wrong is hard for us. So be honest. Do not believe your child is without sin.

Number Ten: **Finally, leave your child with God.** After you have gone through all the parenting principles, been the best parents and have prayed with all your might for them, finally, leave your children with God. God gave them a wonderful and terrible thing. What is it? Free will, a choice. They can choose right or wrong, no matter how much you have put into them. Don't let it break up, hurt, damage, or dampen your marriage. Ultimately, we need to leave our children with God.

## Parenting Principles

1 Don't correct each other in front of the kids.
2 Remember you are the balance for them.
3 Present a singular front.
4 Don't be your child's favorite.
5 Don't have a favorite child.
6 Include the children in the fight resolution.
7 The motivation is restoration not punishment.
8 Never be hesitant to say "I'm sorry."
9 Do not believe your child is without sin.
10 Leave your children with God.

Here in our first maxim, we have been discussing recognizing your bride's need to first be a woman. We looked at her greatest needs. There are five: affection, expression, communion, attraction and union. We talked about allowing for our differences. We considered six different ways we can express our love for our wives: Material Love, Verbal Love, Listening Love, Loyal Love, Sacrificial Love and finally Friendship Love. Our wives, long before we were married, were women. Release your wife into the glory and uniqueness of her womanhood.

# Chapter 2

# Lovers Express
# Their Love

## Lovers express their love.

When you go down to the work place, somebody will say, "Oh, I really like my secretary." Everybody seems to think that's cool. But you say, "I care about my wife." "I love my husband." They look at you like what's wrong with you, and what is the answer? Nothing is wrong with me. I'm on very solid ground.

Song of Solomon 1:9-10, 'To me, my darling, you are like my mare among the chariots of Pharaoh. Your cheeks are lovely with ornaments, your neck with strings of beads.'

I think this scripture has gotten a lot of bad press. He is not saying that his wife is an old gray mare. That is really not what is happening. He is talking here about the war chariots of Pharaoh. They imported these chariots up from Egypt into Israel. In fact, getting just one was extremely difficult. They were ominously powerful, tremendously expensive, and you had to have all kinds of political connections just to own **one**. It was the tank of the day. If you were an infantry man or foot soldier with a charging chariot coming at you, you were in trouble! Any king would be an extremely powerful force in a region if he had a war chariot. Now if you had ten of them, you really were somebody to be reckoned with. If you had a hundred, you literally could rule the nations around you. Solomon had 1,200! It took twelve thousand support troops and three whole chariot cities just to house this massive arsenal of war machines. Solomon controlled the trade routes north and south, east and west, in the center of the world. By the way, he levied all the tariffs and taxes and got opulently wealthy off them. At this point in history Israel was on the ascension. David and Solomon expanded their domain from 5,000 square miles to 50,000 square miles in one generation. That is a massive increase in land mass and in kingdom domain.

Now Solomon's war chariots were all driven by steeds. He is here comparing his bride and calling her the mare among all these steeds. In other words, he is saying, "My wife, when you compare her to all other women, they are like male horses." All comparisons in the *Song of Solomon* are positive. It is not, "You look almost as good as my secretary" or "If you could just look like this lady on television or this gal in the magazine," Don't do that. **All comparisons are positive**.

> All comparisons are positive.

Song of Solomon 1:13-14, '**My beloved is to me a cluster of henna blossoms in the vineyards of Engedi.**'

Let me describe the vineyards of Engedi. When you are standing in Engedi in Israel and you are looking out, in front of you is the

Dead Sea. The Dead Sea is dead, I mean dead. The water temperature gets up to 200°F at the bottom of the sea. There is not a fish living in there, not even a plant. There is nothing, just empty fluid. One doesn't swim in the Dead Sea; one bobs in the Dead Sea. So, standing there, looking out from Engedi, in front of you is the Dead Sea. If you turn around and look in the other direction, you see behind you the Judean wilderness. There is a little bit of shrubbery and grass, but basically not much happening. It is arid and dry, but Engedi is an oasis. There are date palms and banana trees. The oasis is filled with flowers and the air is filled with a wonderful fragrance. It's a beautiful place, Engedi.

So here in scripture when it says '**My beloved is as the vineyards of Engedi**,' what's happening? In front of you is the Dead Sea. That is Monday morning when the coffee maker is broken. It's trying to get to work and you have a flat tire. It's getting to work with the same old employees and the same old boss. It's just **life**. Behind you is the Judean wilderness. Anybody who has been married for more than two or three days has some issues, some things they have been through. They have some things behind them, some dryness, or arid places, some

> Marriage is meant to be a place of approval, growth, honor and friendship.

things they would rather just let go and not remember. In other words, marriage is meant to be a place of approval, growth, honor, friendship and companionship, "Engedi." All these things are meant to fill our marriages.

Song of Solomon 1:15, **'How beautiful you are, my darling, how beautiful you are! Your eyes are like doves.'**

It's the most amazing thing. We always watch couples when they are in public. So many couples don't look at each other. They will come greet their friends, they will say hi to other people. They will talk to their buddies. But it's like there is this invisible wall between them; they are very careful not to make eye contact with their mate. Look into your spouse's eyes for a long time, try three seconds. Now for some couples that is a very long time. Some couples cannot even look into each other's eyes for three seconds. It not only enhances your relationship. It can be a pleasant experience.

Song of Solomon 2:1 (bride speaking), **'I am the rose of Sharon, the lily of the valleys.'** (In the Hebrew it's feminine.)

If the Shulammite is saying this, is she bragging? Not at all. She's not boasting; she is stating her glory and beauty in God. Ladies, think, "I am the rose of Sharon, the lily of the valleys." It probably feels good to contemplate that, and well it should. It is so important that a woman feel good about her mind, her body, her future, her hopes, her dreams.

Now when you see Solomon and the Shulammite, where are they when it says 'cedars, cypresses, valleys' (Song of Solomon 1:17)? Are they watching TV? No. They are outside. They are taking a walk. In fact, you might want to turn the television off occasionally. The average Westerner watches forty-two hours of television a week. It is not going to break the tube to occasionally turn it off. Go for a stroll together.

> The average Westerner watches forty-two hours of television a week.

Song of Solomon 2:2, 'Like a lily among the thorns, So is my darling among the maidens.'

Who is the lily? His wife. Who are the thorns? The other ladies. **All comparisons are positive**.

## Public Interaction Cautions

Let me give you three interaction cautions when you are in the public forum. You want to be cautious when you are in the public forum that, first, you are not embarrassing your spouse. Public embarrassment, watch it. Number two is public degradation or public "put downs." You do not want to bring up past hurts, past issues, and share them in the public forum. It is not the place to get even with each other. Number three is the caution about public side taking. Don't take sides against your spouse in the public forum. Now here is the trick on this one, even if they are wrong! Because so often, they **are** wrong. But don't take sides against your spouse publicly. Publicly you should be able to feel safe and secure with each other. You should not have to worry about being degraded in public. Bring honor to each other when with others.

---

**Cautions**
Public embarrassment
Public "put downs"
Public side taking.

---

Song of Solomon 2:3b, 'In his shade I took great delight and sat down, and his fruit was sweet to my taste.'

'His fruit was sweet to my taste.' That's the *naphach*, that's breath. In other words, guys, brush your teeth; have fresh breath. You want to take showers more often than you might otherwise be inclined to. We want to watch our personal hygiene. It's important that the *naphach* is sweet.

## Great Palace Complex

Song of Solomon 2:4, **'He has brought me to *his* banquet hall, and his banner over me is love.'**

Let's use our minds and our imaginations to picture the banquet hall of Solomon. It was stunning. We are going to go into the Great Palace Complex.

As you would come into that first room, you would be walking across marble stone work. Now around you were massive gold shields. They were literally tingling and alive with light. There were two hundred gold shields all around you about six feet tall and about three hundred smaller beaten gold shields above that. The Phoenicians had developed a window system, which Solomon used, where the sunlight would come in and reflect back and forth. It would blind you with light. With forty-five feet high cedar beams set in three columns, this whole first room was called the Palace of the Forest of Lebanon. It was like a living forest.

As you walked out of that room, you would then come into a retaining room, a second room, where the whole walls were bas reliefs, carvings by the finest craftsmen in the world. Your nostrils were filled with sandalwood and many other exotic fragrances. It would sometimes take two and three thousand pounds of petals pressed into liquid to make a single ounce of the ointment that permeated the room. Your mind and senses were opulently stretched here in the Hall of Pillars.

Walking into the final inner chamber, you would literally sink downward into leopard skins and numerous exotic animal hides from far away places, spread across the floor. The attendants were all clad in gold and purple. In fact, there were live peacocks walking free and live apes in the room. Again across the wall were bas reliefs, while sandalwood fragrances were filling your nostrils.

However, all of that would dim and you would hardly see it. Why? Because in front of you, was The Throne! The Bible says **'nothing like it was made for any other kingdom'** (1 Kings 10:20). There were six sets of carved ivory lions as you made your way up on these steps, up higher and higher, closer and closer to the throne itself. As you finally reached the top step, the lions were not carved. They were *alive*! Within inches of your legs, they were chained, I'm happy to say. But breathing hot breath on your legs were live lions!

Even that would dim because of him sitting on the throne of polished gold. The eyes looking at you were the eyes of the wisest man that ever walked this earth, excepting our Lord Jesus. Literally the anointing of divine wisdom was on this man. Those eyes were looking at you with reception and care, tenderness and love.

This is a type of what it will be like some day for the Christian to stand before the throne of God and look into the eyes of Jesus. Those eyes will meet your eyes with reception, love, care and tenderness.

The Shulammite was getting a little weak-kneed. I probably would too.

Song of Solomon 2:5, **'Sustain me with raisin cakes, refresh me with apples, because I am lovesick.'**

This kind of dialog is almost lost in our culture. A generation ago, 1.2 million couples sought private therapy for their marriages.

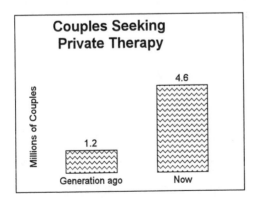

Now it has reached 4.6 million couples seeking private therapy[3]. That does not even count the couples that are in the middle of personal agony that are not wanting to spend $150 an hour for private therapy. We are dealing with a major issue. The pop culture of pseudo psychology changes again and again. Even when I was at Oxford University, there were twenty-one doctoral candidates in our class, and we could hardly agree on anything. The Bible is the standard that can speak to our homes.

Song of Solomon 2:6, '*Let his left hand be under my head and his right hand embrace me.*'

So the Shulammite is daydreaming here about making love. With whom? Her husband! She is daydreaming about making love with him alone, and it is good. Sexuality, sin twists it, Satan wants to warp it. But this was God's idea. Where? In **marriage**, not extra-marriage, not pre-marriage. In the context of marriage God means for us to be wonderfully fulfilled.

Lovers express their love.

# Chapter 3

# Dwell on
# Your Lover's Good

# Dwell on your lover's good.

Is that easy? No!

Song of Solomon 2:8-9, 'Listen! My beloved! Behold, he is coming, climbing on the mountains, leaping on the hills! 'My beloved is like a gazelle or a young stag. Behold, he is standing behind our wall, he is looking through the windows, he is peering through the lattice.'

Solomon's wife is laying it on here pretty thick. Look at these active verbs. She is seeing him "coming, climbing, leaping, peering, looking, standing." She is thinking positive thoughts. Now she doesn't say, "Will you quit staring out that window?" What was Solomon like around the house, by the way? He had all these worldwide duties. She doesn't snap, "You are so inept when it comes to the home chores. You're so involved with your trade routes." She is really trying to dwell on the positive here.

Now ladies, can you think of positive things about your man? It is no fair pleading "temporary insanity" related to your wedding day. There was nothing wrong with you; you just need to stir up the good. I want you to think of three positive things about your husband. You might think, "Great taste in women!" Maybe he is caring, maybe he is understanding, maybe he is a good father, maybe he is a good provider. The point is find the good.

Seventy percent of all divorces happen in the first five years of marriage. Anybody married five years or more? Nice job. Anybody married less than five years — take hope, it is possible!

*Song of Solomon* says, **'Catch the foxes for us, the little foxes that are ruining the vineyards.'** This is talking about these fifteen inch high little Fennet foxes, these nasty little critters. Here is what would happen. People had vineyards in ancient Israel, and their vineyards were the main sustenance for a number of families. In Israel, around 1000 BC, the fox would come out and take a bite, just a little nibble on the main vine. One nibble one night, two nibbles the next night, maybe just a nibble the next. That doesn't seem like much, except what happened is that the life would begin to flow out of the vine and the grapes would drop to the ground too soon. We think, "No big deal; go down to the local supermarket and get some more grapes." Not if it is 1,000 BC. In fact, a family could literally starve to death by the damage done by these little foxes. Nibble, nibble, nibble.

Our marriages function the same kind of way. Little issue, no big deal; several little issues, still no big deal. Little bite here, little bite there, by themselves they are not much of a problem. But you put enough of these together and soon you find some of the life-flow going out of your relationship. Now this could be anything. It could be whether you roll or squeeze the toothpaste — "Got to be rolled." "No, squeezed!" This could be using the TV remote — "Mine." "No, mine!" This could be any subject, any little thing. Hair curlers for one guy was his "fox." It drove him crazy to see his wife always in curlers. Now I want you to think of a couple of "foxes."Think of some little issues, some little foxes. Now don't go after the **lions and leopards.'** We will deal with those later. These are the little issues, the little foxes. For one husband, he was always calling his wife, "HONEY," with teeth clenched. The kids all thought he was swearing at their mother until they grew up a little bit and found that it was just a term of endearment he was misusing. It could be any issue. The issue here is that you are after the "fox" not the mate. Personal attacks can easily put one on the defensive, but if it's the fox we're after, it's much easier to respond to, both for the one who has the issue and the mate who is fox hunting.

## Successful Communication Keys

As we spend time with each other, we need to have it be **effective** time. Let me give you some successful communication keys. Here are six keys for communicating in your marriage. By the way, these keys will work well with your kids. They will work well with your employer, your employees, or your friends. Although we're applying them to your marriage, they will still work on any relationship. I want to give you three Talking Keys and three

Listening Keys. It's important to be both a good listener and an effective talker.

## *Talking Keys*

### TALK TOGETHER

Talking Key number 1: **Talk Together.** When you are communicating, when you are having time together, you are looking to have your communication bring you together rather than separate you. One might think, that's obvious, and **it is** obvious except that so often we don't do it. It is important that we get on the **same** subject. The same subject for a short period of time is much more effective than different interests dividing you in your communication. So often couples are talking but they are not finding each other at all. They are not talking together, but they are on different web pages, talking about totally different things. You say, "Yes, I'm listening." Are we listening? Or are you just waiting to speak about what you want to talk about. So **talk together**. Remember to wait for the right time. We do not want to wait until the baby is screaming, the doorbell is ringing, the dog just kicked over the bowl and there is a big mess on the floor and then say "Darling can we have a nice quiet talk now?" What is the answer? "No! Absolutely not!" You want to do it at the right time, and you also want to be careful that your talk is bringing you together. Be careful with each other. I think so often we forget that just because we are married, it does not mean our spouse is a place where we dump all the garbage we collect. We think "well we are married so I will say whatever I want to say in our marriage." If you want to have a successful marriage that lasts and you want to have your talk bring you **together**, then realize that your marriage is not the local dumpster.

Perhaps you have had a bad dream or even a nightmare. When you wake up in the morning, don't let it be the first thing your spouse hears in the morning, the gory details. To tell them you've just had an awful dream and let them know you need a few minutes to shake it off is great, but to pull them into the depression of the nightmare is counterproductive. The former brings you together, the latter separates you. Have your talk be attracting not repelling. **Talk together**.

### TALK TRUTHFULLY

Talking Key number 2: **Talk Truthfully**. You do not want to open up a subject that you are not going to finish. The conversation can go something like this: "I can't stand the way you do that!" "Do what?" "Oh never mind." Be careful not to just leave these things dangling out there, bringing up a subject you are not going to finish. You want your talk to be truthful, conclusive and you also want to avoid superlatives. "You **never** are sensitive to me!" Now maybe he is not being sensitive and has not been for almost two weeks. But "always," "never?" Try to pull those words out of your marital vocabulary. Avoid the superlatives and talk truthfully. This means to share what is bothering you, but remember that your spouse is not a mind reader. Your spouse still needs to have communication and to be talked to **truthfully**.

## TALK TO BE TAUGHT

Talking Key number 3: **Talk to Be Taught**. This is a whole new way of talking. Strive to talk to **learn**, rather than always to teach. In other words we are looking to learn. We are looking to actively communicate. We are not just looking for a platform to educate. We do not just want a stage in our marriage where we are just verbalizing, but a place where we can be taught. Consider avoiding selective input. "Oh my boss, what a rat. I have to work until six o'clock every night" you tell your spouse, "and I used to get off at five o'clock. Now I have to work until six, and every Tuesday, (which is our night together). I've got to go in and labor under the rodent." Then your spouse says, "Oh what a rat." And you get just the response you are looking for, but you forget to mention that the boss also gave you a 40% raise. Now, maybe for a 40% salary jump you would be willing to work the extra hour. But at least avoid the **selective** input. You want to give the **whole** story. You want to be truthful, and you want to talk to be taught. Prov. 9:8 says, '**Reprove a wise man and he will be wiser still.**'

# *Listening Keys*

### LISTEN WITH INTEREST

Listening Key number 1: **Listen with Interest**. Put your heart into it. This means actually let your spouse know you care about what they are talking about. Let them feel you are truly interested in them. When you listen with interest, have your eyes listen too. Look at them and actually show them that you care; give them your undivided attention. This means **don't interrupt**.

Have you been interrupted? If one of you is a little more talkative, (and there is usually one in every marriage), then the talkative one is the one that needs to take note. It is not what you are publicly, but how you are privately that is at issue here. We may act one way publicly and respond privately in a totally different way. If you both want to start sharing something at the same time and one of you is a little more talkative, that's the one that takes the step back. If you both start sharing at the same time, relent, talker. It really does help to even it out, so your spouse will begin to come forward. A person that has not really drawn their mate out and developed in their mate what needs to be enhanced in their personhood is the lesser for their dominance.

### LISTEN WITH INTENSITY

Listening Key number 2: **Listen with Intensity**. In other words, listen with your soul. This means feel what they feel while are they sharing. So many couples waste time when they are with each other. Think about when you see a couple out for a breakfast and one of them is reading the newspaper and the other one is reading a magazine. Are they having breakfast with each other? No! They are having breakfast with the newspaper and the magazine. Put the newspaper down. Put the magazine down. Make the most of your time with each other and listen with intensity. How can you secure your mate more? How can you strengthen them, help them, enhance their maturity, reach them?

### LISTEN WITH INSIGHT

Listening Key number 3: **Listen with Insight**. Learn your spouse. Do you know her/him? Draw your spouse out and learn who they are. This is going to take more than a couple of weeks. It is going to take a whole life together. As you develop your marriage, you can gain more insight into your spouse. This gives you great power for good in their lives, power to be the key to helping them fulfill their calling in God.

---

## Successful Communication Keys

### Talking Keys

Talk Together
Talk Truthfully
Talk to Be Taught

### Listening Keys

Listen with Interest
Listen with Intensity
Listen with Insight

---

## Purpose of Communication

What is the motive of all this? Why even communicate? To be friends, for starters. My wife calls it companionship love. I call it friendship love. We are just coming from two angles saying the same thing. But be friends and companions. You are going to be married for a lifetime, so make the most of it. You might as well be buddies. Work on your friendship. **Friendship love.**

## Marital Goals

Do something with this thing called **marriage.**

Have **marital goals.** You don't just want to live in the same building and vegetate. We want to do something with this thing called

**marriage**. We want it to go somewhere, so have some marital goals. Our daughter Christy, when she was seven years old, was so afraid of math that Sandy and I were really getting worried. You could say 3 × 7 and Christy would freeze. You might as well have said, "There is a huge monster standing there behind you." There were just too many numbers. She could not do it. So we made up a little game. We began to work with this thing. Sandy and I prayed for her and did everything we could to help her with math. We decided to make this a **marital goal**. If Christy could say 3 × 7 = 21, Daddy would jump. There was no real rationale to that, but Dad would be a frog. Sometimes I would be up in front of a group and Christy would whisper "3 × 7 = 21" and the speaker would jump. She got a lot of kicks out of this thing. We hired a tutor as well, costing us five dollars a week, which was a lot of money twenty years ago. The tutor came in forty-five minutes a week to work with Christy on math. I will never forget the day she came running out of the room where he was teaching her screaming, "Mommy, Daddy, I got math!" I said, "You got math? What do you mean?" And she said, "Yep, got math." The tutor came out and said that he gave her three questions and she got them all right. I said "was one of them 3 × 7 = 21?" He said, "Yes as a matter of fact, why?" Christy, as an adult, was hired by one of the largest private schools in the city of Orlando, Florida, to teach junior high math! Marital goal accomplished! In our marriages we should have a bunch of these **goals**. Maybe it is just to get away for a long weekend alone with each other or move toward debt retirement. But have goals, a bunch of them, and be after reaching them together.

## Forgiveness

I was taking a tutorial at Oxford University from Dr. Davies. Prof. Davies was the former editor of the Oxford English Dictionary. He was instructing on some subject that I've long forgotten. But at one point he mentioned he had been married **twenty-one years**. I thought, I'm going to go ask him, "Why the longevity? Why such a long marriage?" I went up to him after class and said, "Dr. Davies, I noticed you mentioned you had been married twenty-one years. What do you owe such a long marriage to?" I figured I was going to get some huge answer, the anthropological and sociological interface of some kind of cultural interaction. Do you know what he did? He looked at me and he said one word. He said "forgiveness." **Forgiveness**! That said so much in one word. Marriage should be **filled** with forgiveness.

You wake up in the morning and look in the mirror and think, "I need to work on this thing quickly." We need some fast forgiveness while we fix up before our spouse sees us. Let me encourage us to have forgiveness working in our heart all day long, with the kids, shopping, car pooling, all the

> Having understanding, forgiveness and sensitivity

multitude of marital interactions. . . having understanding, forgiveness and sensitivity with our mate.

Dwell on your lover's good. That's not easy. Let's exercise our mind, our heart, our will to dwell on our lover's good. However, it's simply a happier way to live.

# 3 — Dwell On Your Lover's Good

# Chapter 4

# Never Give Up on Your Love

## Never give up on your love.

When you go down to your local drive through burger place, you order a quarter pounder with cheese. But they give you a quarter pounder. You say, "Now wait a minute, I ordered a quarter pounder with cheese." So you give the burger back and say, "I paid for a quarter pounder **with** cheese. I'd like the quarter pounder **with** cheese." You go out to buy a color TV with a remote, and the store gives you a black and white set that you have to manually turn the channels. You say again, "Now wait a minute. I paid for a **color** TV **with** a remote." You pick out and sign for a blue truck and the dealer gives you a red sedan. You say, "Hold on, this isn't what I signed up to make payments on." We have taken this kind of "turn it around" mentality that is so prevalent in our culture and misapplied it to our marriage. When we don't get the "quarter pounder with **cheese**" that you **ordered** the first time, then we have a trade it in kind of mentality. It may work for a cheeseburger, to turn it around, but certainly the covenant of marriage is not meant to be handled so lightly. Rather than the trade in, don't give up on your marriage; make it work.

Song of Solomon 3:1, 'On my bed night after night I sought him whom my soul loves; I sought him but did not find him.'

She says, "I sought him." In this passage and the ones that are coming, four times she is saying "I sought him, I sought him." She is seeking after her husband. Marriage does not end on wedding day. That is where it begins! It is life long pursuing and seeking each other. After nearly thirty years of marriage, I am starting to understand and know my Sandy. Marriage is a pursuit of union, a travail of love, a struggle of mentally, physically and spiritually becoming one.

> Marriage is a pursuit of union, a travail of love, a struggle of mentality, physically and spiritually becoming one.

Recently, we have seen the most difficult thing happening, related to the Internet and marriages. A new phenomenon has been occurring. All across this country, marriages are breaking up via the Internet because people have "found someone" else out there in cyberspace. That is someone they have never even spoken to or never even met, and they are literally leaving their spouses for a person that they have "found." Now what does this show us? It actually blazes at us in living color the importance of **communication** in marriage. You remove the constraints and all the hassles, and are just able to talk, and you can "find" someone. Let's remove the interference and seek out that someone in our marriages.

Would you be willing to give 5% of your time into the most important relationship you have in the world, (outside your relationship with God), which is to your spouse? Most people say, "All right, no problem. I will invest 5% into my marriage, as long as I have 95% to go fishing, play football, go shopping, enjoy my friends, go to work, eat, sleep, do everything else. I'll give 5%."

Now this is what I would like you to do. I want you to begin by spending one night a week with each other[4]. Take a night that is your night. Not one night a week with each other and the kids. No. Not spending a night with each other and the in-laws? Definitely not. Not even the night with each other and the TV set. No. Take a night that is **your spouse night**. One might think, "Well, I can't spend a night because I work nights." All right, take a morning. Find some time.

Spend one day a month together. Find a day a month that is your day with each other, a day you will spend together. Plan a day trip or maybe an overnight. Take a day that is **your day**.

Set aside one long weekend a year to spend together. However, if it has been four, five, six, maybe going on seven years and you haven't taken one piece of time that is your time with each other, something is going

> Give 5% of your time into the most important relationship you have in the world.

to begin to ebb out of your marriage, guaranteed. Work on it in your marriage to get a chunk of time that is going to be your time away with each other.

I talked to an elderly man the other day. He had been married fifty-four years, and I asked him the same question I asked Dr. Davies in England. "Wow, a fifty-four year marriage. What do you owe such a long marriage to?" Do you know what he said to me? "T'wern't no reason to leave her . . ." That's not a bad answer. Think about it. He was saying nothing was so big, nothing was so huge, nothing was so critical that he was going to blow out of that marriage. T'wern't no reason to leave her. You know, we in this culture are almost looking for exits. "Well this is not really convenient" or "Not exactly what I was looking for." We were too young when we started or we didn't know what we were getting into. Who does! We are breaking what God wants to pull together. "Never give up on your love."

Song of Solomon 3:4, '**I found him whom my soul loves; I held on to him and would not let him go.**'

Now does this mean this couple had total marital bliss? No, not at all, it means on one issue they had found each other, they had come to something. So it's a building process. And we are going somewhere together.

We were at the Western Wall, actually underneath the Wailing Wall in Jerusalem when they first opened up a brand new archeological dig around 1980. We had the opportunity to walk down at night underneath the historic site to this dig that had only been opened up for three days. We were crawling along down underneath rubble. Two hundred feet of it was above us. Garbage would be more accurate because it was **dripping**. We were crawling along about a quarter mile underground past all these old Herodian stones, finished in 4 BC.

Suddenly as we traveled down to the bed rock, there that night, there were four stones that were different, **sixty and eighty** ton stones! We had an Israeli army captain as our guide, who pulled out his pocket knife and said, "Watch this." He tried to get his pocket knife between the stones, but they were so perfectly cut, he couldn't even get his knife between them. I was running my hands along these stones, my eyes are getting bigger and bigger, and I said, "Solomonic, are these first temple stones?" I will never forget his answer, he said, "According to our research, we believe that to be the case." My heart was pounding . . . "I'm touching first temple stones," that hadn't been uncovered since the time of Titus in 70 AD when the Roman Legions dropped Jerusalem in flames and ashes, 3,000 year old hand cut First Temple stones!

We went a little bit further and there was an entranceway; they had only cleared about a yard back into it. I will never forget that archway. It was totally covered with dirt and rocks. When I enquired, the guide said, "Well that is a doorway, we believe, into a retaining room. We believe that there was a room back in there that the priests would use to hold articles for the temple mount above. In the back of it we think we are going to find a passage that will go up to the temple area above, up to the Holy place where the priests would minister." My mind was racing as I thought, "Titus, the catapults, Jerusalem burning, the priests trying to save some candelabra or some of the articles of the Temple. What is in that room?" I wanted to say, "Does anyone have a spoon so I can dig back there another six inches to see what might stick out?" Regrettably, political trouble developed, and the decision was made to take out the shovels and fill the whole thing in. But we were there for the first time it had been uncovered in 2,000 years.

## Marital Foundation Stones

I believe down at the bedrock of our marriages, there are the perfectly cut stones of God's purpose, God's will, God's blessing and His plan for our marriages. One thinks, "But we've been through so many things, all the rubble, all the junk, all the problems." But God cares more about your marriage than you do! One ponders, "But that's impossible; I really care about this marriage." God is the one who created marriage and He cares even more about it than we do.

Song of Solomon 3:5, 'I adjure you, O daughters of Jerusalem, by the gazelles or by the hinds of the field, that you will not arouse or awaken my love, until she pleases.'

She pleases where? In marriage. The gazelle is a graceful, wonderful animal, able to go into the high, high places, with care and sure footing. Have you ever been in the middle of a fuss and suddenly you forget what you are fussing about? Do you know what that pause is? I think that's God's grace saying, "Slow down, easy. I've created marriage. Take it easy on each other." God is bringing that grace as a gazelle, that **divine pause** in our marriage.

In a society and a culture that is giving up on everything, trading it back in, let's make this commitment to marriage. "I will never give up on our love."

# Chapter 5

# God Has Ordained Your Marriage

We hear this all the time. "I'm not sure I found the right guy." Or "I'm not sure it was the right gal I married." Or "We did not really know what we were getting into." None of us knows what we are getting into. When we take the orientation off ourselves and put it on Him, it changes our whole perspective.

## God has ordained your marriage.

Song of Solomon 3:6-8, '**What is this coming up from the wilderness like columns of smoke, perfumed with myrrh and frankincense, with all scented powders of the merchant?** [7]**Behold, it is the** *traveling* **couch of Solomon; sixty mighty men around it, of the mighty men of Israel.** [8]**All of them are wielders of the sword, expert in war; each man has his sword at his side, guarding against the terrors of the night.'**

Now this is talking about the traveling couch, or palanquin throne of Solomon. We know quite a bit about the wedding day of Solomon from the scriptures as well as a number of Jewish writings.

Basically, there was this teenage shepherd girl. Her brothers were upset at her saying something like this, "It's your turn to go out and tend the flock for a while. We have been sun burned enough.

You go out and get cooked." So she went out and was tending the family flock. Solomon would travel once a year around his whole domain. All the kings at this time did this, to show their power and make sure the kingdom knew they were still in control.

Solomon had set up his tents or his "curtains," as they were called, there in southern Lebanon. The region was part of his domain, conquered by his father and expanded by Solomon through all the treaties he had enacted. She had seen the king's 'curtains,' the glistening of the gold threading! Evidently Solomon had come out and seen this shepherd girl. They had evidently fallen in love, and then decided they wanted to get married. So he would have gone to her father, which would have been the normal custom of the day, to establish the dowry. Imagine that dowry? Lucky Dad.

Solomon then went back to Jerusalem without her to prepare a place for her. Now the analogies are huge of Christ going to heaven, preparing a place to receive us, His Bride. It would be about a three day, two night journey for the King to return to Jerusalem. For three months he then prepared this incredible palanquin / couch to go up to Lebanon to receive her and bring her down to the capital for their wedding day. You can imagine his preparation, all the gold and splendor of the palanquin. I'm sure he took a few handfuls of rubies and for sparkle a couple handfuls of diamonds. I don't know what your wedding was like, but this thing was going to be big time!

Finally, he sent the palanquin up north with his crack troops, these massive guards, sixty of them. He had six hundred in his private guard. Here were the best of the best. Some of them were probably David's mighty men, passed down to his son, Solomon. They were coming closer and closer, carrying this throne / couch to the little village of Shulam. You can imagine the excitement of that hamlet as she had her best dress all ready to go, as her brothers come running in, "They are coming. We can see them out in the wilderness! We can see their dust." See her walking out on her dad's arm, and he is so proud. Of course she kisses her mom good bye and then hugs her dad. The chief guard comes up and all the salutations take place and he would help her up into the palanquin. As she pushes the lace back, all these intoxicating perfumes and fragrances come out, all the sparkle and glitter. I'm sure she reached in and picked up Solomon's gifts and whispered out to her girl friends, "All these stones in here, I think some of them might be real diamonds!"

This was a big jump. A teenage shepherd girl, then queen of Israel! Big leap. We are lost without Christ, then we come to Him. It's a big jump, isn't it? Sure it is. So then they would turn and make their way out into the wilderness. These guards would carry this opulent palanquin, guarding through the terrors of the wilderness, back on the journey to Jerusalem.

As you go through marriage, there is a beast, there is a monster, who wants to attack your home. And that beast's name is **Divorce**. I think that word ought to be a swear word in the Christian home. We have never used the word "divorce" in our home related to our relationship. We don't want to give it power.

We all hear about the 49% divorce rate, and that is tragic. But, that statistic is for marriage as a whole. It doesn't reveal what the divorce rate is for second time marriages. The

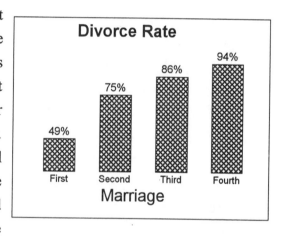

**Divorce Rate**

49% First
75% Second
86% Third
94% Fourth

Marriage

divorce rate for second time marriages is not 49%; it is **75%**. Seventy-five percent of all second time marriages are going, statistically, to end in divorce. Third time marriages have a divorce rate of 86%. Of all third time marriages, statistically, 86% are going to end in divorce! You see where this is going quickly. Fourth time marriages have an almost complete failure rate.

Statistically, 94% of all fourth time marriages are going to end in divorce!

I am not bringing these statistics by way of condemnation. The opposite. I am saying one word, **STOP**. You are on your third marriage? Stop right there. Work this one out. You are on your fourth marriage? OK, let's make this one sparkle, let's make this one shine! You are on your first marriage, Stay put.

We hear all the time, "Well, I don't know. I've learned a lot. The next one will be so much easier." Don't you believe it! Statistically that is completely erroneous. It only gets more difficult. So wherever you are, stop and make this one a success.

God cares about your marriage. As a matter of fact, **God has ordained your marriage**. Even beyond that, God has ordained **marriage**. This has been proven statistically. A fascinating study recently came out by Dr. Waite[5], at the University of Chicago, a fifteen-year comprehensive study following singles versus marrieds. If you look at the married woman's life span versus the single, the married woman, statistically, is going to live 1,600 days longer than the single gal, just by staying married! Not a bad trade off. But it's not so for the guy. The guy will not live 1,600 days longer than the single man. The married man is going to live 3,500 days longer than the single guy, just by being married! **Ten years** longer life than the single guy!

When the Bible says, '𝐈𝐭 𝐢𝐬 𝐧𝐨𝐭 𝐠𝐨𝐨𝐝 𝐟𝐨𝐫 𝐦𝐚𝐧 𝐭𝐨 𝐛𝐞 𝐚𝐥𝐨𝐧𝐞,' (Gen. 2:18) the Bible means it. The study went on to talk about median household wealth. There is a mentality that the single out there is having all the fun. He has his sports car, his stereos and CD players, while the poor bedraggled married has to buy clothes for the kids, pay the insurance bills and take care of all the financial burdens. He is weighted down while, supposedly, the single is out there with all these material wonders. Guess what, this is not true! The median household wealth of the single man in the United States, when you count his cars, his stereos, his CD players, his big screen TV's and everything you can think of, is $32,000, while the married is $134,200!

The study went on to find out who was having all the "fun." There is this mentality that "weekends are made for Michelob." Guess what, they are not; they are made for God. There is a conception of the single guy, and the single gal are out there in bars and running around and having all the fun. Let me tell you, it is a deception. Behind the bedroom door, we're the ones having all the fun! It is about a three to one ratio in the marrieds' favor. We're the ones having **the most fun** and under God's blessing.

So if you want to be healthier, wealthier and wiser, get married and **stay** married! When we say God has ordained marriage, He sure has. **He has ordained *your* marriage**.

To be happily married and stay married, let's go through some conflict resolution. Let's work through an acrostic, PROBLEM.

## Problem Solving

## Prayer

**P** is **Prayer**. If you want to solve your problems, bring prayer into your marriage. The studies show that only 10-15% of all churchgoing couples pray together. I gasped when I first heard that statistic. Only 10-15%. That means that 90% of all **churchgoing couples** don't pray together. Where does that leave the rest of the world? So let's bring prayer into our marriages. Here is a marriage prayer, "Help." Or you can do a long one, "Help, God." Those will work. You may not have time for anything else but just "Help." Bring the Lord into your marriage. I am not saying get into the middle of a full force fight and then say, "Let's have a nice quiet, long time of prayer." That's not what I am saying. But when you **do** pray, you want to pray **for** each other, not **at** each other. Don't pray, "God break this woman." "God smash this guy." Don't pray that way. You want to pray **for** each other and you want to pray **with** each other.

> Pray **for** each other, not **at** each other.

I talked to Ben and Elma. They had been married sixty years. That is diamond anniversary time. I asked, "Why such a long marriage." They said, "We pray together." That is all they would say. "We pray together." They would not let up on the thing. They were giving the whole credit of a sixty-year marriage to the fact they prayed together. Prayer softens us and helps our marriage stay alive.

## Renewing your mind

**R** is **Renewing your mind**. So often we do not want to be changed. We get stuck in our ways. But the scripture talks about renewing your mind. As a matter of fact, it says, 'taking every thought captive to the obedience of Christ' in 2 Corinthians 10:5. We need to get hold of our minds under Christ. So many things can run through them. Are you aware that Satan hates **marriage**? But if you are a Christian, he especially hates **your** marriage. You might as well be walking around with a target on your back. It's true, but we have a great God. Satan loathes your mind dwelling on God and despises your dwelling on positive things related to your home and your spouse. He wants you negative because that is where he lives. Christ lives in the heavenlies; we are to be seated with Him there.

Renewing your mind. This means being sensitive to each other. If

> Sensitivity to each other can go a long way toward marital harmony.

there is sickness in the family, if there has been a death, whatever it is, be sensitive. Be sensitive during the woman's time of the month. I saw a bumper sticker the other day. It said, "Women act once a month like men do daily." That may or may not be true, but sensitivity to each other can go a long way toward marital harmony.

## DON'T MINIMIZE THE PROBLEM

You do not want to **minimize the problem**. A lady was talking to my wife, who was very upset and crying. Sandy was listening to her tell how her husband had been buying gifts for his secretary. She said "It started with some flowers on secretary's day and then perfume and little cards and stuff. Now it had moved to where he was buying her whole outfits." She said, "Not only that, he wasn't doing that for me at all, just for his secretary." My wife said, "Have you brought it to him and told him how much hurt this is bringing to you?" She said, "Yes I have. But here is what he said to me. He said, 'No big deal. We're just friends!'" What was he doing when he said "We're just friends?" He was **minimizing the problem**. He was making less of it than it really was. It was a bigger deal than that. Be careful of minimizing the problem.

## DON'T MAXIMIZE THE PROBLEM

You don't want to **maximize the problem** either. You don't want to minimize it, nor do you want to maximize the problem. We were over at this couple's home for the first time. I had heard that she made great spaghetti and lasagne. It smelled wonderful and I was looking forward to dinner. The husband was out in the dining room trying to set the table. I can never get this straight. If there are three forks, two spoons, two knives, which way does the blade go and on which side of the plate does each piece go? This poor guy was shifting it around, scratching his head. I watched him struggle with it. I guess he got it wrong, because his wife came out of the kitchen, saw what he had done at the table, and growled, "What's this?!" He wheeled on her and snapped, "What's it to you?" Suddenly, boom. They were saying, "You take the bedroom suite, I'll take the living room furniture. You take this kid. I'll take that kid." They started dividing up the whole house right there in front of us. They were taking it to Defcon 1, full scale war. We said, "Now wait a minute. We're talking about a table setting here. We are talking about a fork and a knife placement." But what were they doing? They were **maximizing the problem**. They were taking it to battle stations. Don't push those buttons. **Don't maximize the problem**.

### DON'T MUTE THE PROBLEM

Don't **mute the problem**. We have a way of doing this. We mute our spouse. "My way is the right way; your way is wrong." We muzzle each other. It's not usually a black and white situation. "I'm right. You're wrong." We really need to hear their side. Be sensitive to each other, hearing how you can get through this problem, because the problem belongs to both of you together. There is an old Chinese proverb that says, "Because you have silenced another does not mean you have converted him." How true! Muting your mate may delay the issue but certainly will not solve it.

## DON'T MISS THE PROBLEM

Don't **miss the problem**. I was speaking at a conference, and I will never forget the guy in the front row. I don't know if he had gotten into some poison ivy or what, but he kept scratching. Scratch, scratch. It was driving his wife crazy. She kept whispering, "Stop that; stop that." Finally he figured out a way to scratch without her knowing it. He got out his pen and used it to scratch so she never saw him move his arm. She was there just quietly listening to the conference. Suddenly she looked over and screamed. The pen was open! He had drawn black marks all up and down his arm, all over his shirt. He looked at his arm and realized what he had done and yelped as well. Now he had missed the whole thing. He hadn't seen what he had been doing. You know, a real way to not miss the problem is to see it through whose eyes? Your spouse's eyes. They can see us pretty well. Unless you are very vain, walking around all day with a mirror, your spouse is going to see you a lot more clearly than you see yourself, if you are willing to listen.

# Other's well being

O is the **Other's Well Being**. If someone has told you something like this, "Marriage is a 50:50 proposition," they lied. Marriage is not a 50:50 proposition. It is 100% give, how often? One hundred percent of the time, **by both** spouses or it doesn't work. Why? When you set up a 50:50 deal, "I've done my half, let's see yours," you've set up a conflict, You've set up battle lines. But if you approach it that you are looking to give into the marriage, 100% of the time, 100% of you, it changes the whole perspective. It will begin to soften your marriage and your relationship.

# Building process

B is a **Building Process**. Build on what you have learned from past issues. Don't bring the "old baggage" into the new conflict. Old baggage . . . ? "Remember three months ago you did this and just two years ago I remember when that happened." We bring up the old baggage and drop it on each other. Develop a building process; say things **positively**. Oh, is this important! I talked to a man. "Paul," he said, "last night I had quite a fight with my wife. I know I did the right thing. I just wanted you to hear the story." I knew he was just looking for ammo against his wife. He was just trying to get my name on what he had done. I said, "Well, what happened?" He said, "I'm sure you will agree with what I did. Here's what happened. My wife said she was going out to be with some of her friends and said she would be back at 9:30. It got to be 11:30 at night." I could see his blood pressure rising. I said, "What happened?" He said, "When she came home I told her in no uncertain terms this was never going to happen again." I said, "And her response?" He answered, "Well, she said next time she would be home by 1:30 in the morning." I said, "So it didn't work." He sheepishly replied, "Well, not exactly." I advised him, "You might have wanted to say it a little differently. You might have wanted to say something like this,

> Develop a building process; say things **positively**.

'Dear, you said you would be back at 9:30. When it got on toward 10:00, 10:30, my mind started going and I began to worry about you. I love you and care about you. I did not know if you had been abducted or had broken down along the side of the road. All these things were going through my head. If you don't mind next time just give me a call to let me know you are all right. I really am deeply attached to you. I really want you to be OK." He blankly looked at me and questioned, "Do you think that would have made any difference?" I said, "Yes. I think it might have made all the difference." How we say things to each other is so important. We need to communicate positively and have our marriage be a **building process**.

## Leave it

L is **Let Not the Sun Go Down on Your Wrath**. (Ephesians 4:26) I talked to Carl, who had been married sixteen years. His wife had contracted terminal cancer and died. He remarried and was married to his second wife for twenty-three years. **Double longevity**. I said "Wow, two long marriages. What do you owe such long marriages to?" Do you know what he said? "We never took our fight into the next day." That is a good answer. Never take a fight into the next day.

## End the fight

That brings us to E which is **End the Fight**. Don't resurrect it. I think some of the worst fights are things where you have already come to some resolution. Then you bring up an old conflict and throw it in your spouse's face. You are asking for trouble. You go deeper and deeper, round and round. Let's fight redemptively. Fight within the covenant. He looks better with a head on; leave it on. I think it's important that we do end the fight. You want to come to something. Maybe it's 11:30 at night, going on quarter of twelve. One spouse says, "I've got to work tomorrow. We have been talking about this for an hour and a half and haven't come to anything." And the last thing you hear from your spouse is "I've had it with you. You're just a jerk." Then you go to sleep and that statement lands right in your stomach. You wake up the next morning. "All right, let's go at it again . . ."

Or the last thing you hear from your spouse is something like this, "I want you to know, although we are in the middle of this issue and we haven't gotten anywhere, I'm committed to this marriage, and I'm committed to you. We are going to trust God to get us through." And then go to sleep. It'll be a brighter morning.

## Mighty God

We do have a mighty God. He's mighty at healing hearts and mighty at marriage making. He cares for you and your spouse. Your marriage means more to Him even than it does to you. It is He that has brought you together and it is He that will keep you together. Align yourself with His gentleness toward your mate. Forgive as He's forgiven you. Pray as Christ prays for His bride the church. Most of all, have your marriage reflect the glory of a Mighty God. "God has ordained your marriage" for Himself and for His honor.

---

**Problem Solving**

**P** rayer
**R** enewing your mind
**O** ther's well being
**B** uilding process
**L** et not the sun
**E** nd the fight
**M** ighty God

---

# Chapter 6

# Praise for Your Bride Is Becoming

## Praise for your bride is becoming.

Out on the highway the other day I saw a giant billboard, with one word on it, "Beautiful." Right below it was a picture of a submarine sandwich! We will praise anything, won't we? That's a praise, "**Beautiful** . . . submarine sandwich." We will state, "What a lovely car." "What an exquisite fishing rod." We will praise about anything. But read how Solomon is praising his bride here.

Song of Solomon 4:1-3, 5, 7 ¹**How beautiful you are, my darling, how beautiful you are! Your eyes are *like* doves behind your veil; your hair is like a flock of goats that have descended from Mount Gilead. ²Your teeth are like a flock of *newly* shorn ewes which have come up from *their* washing, all of which bear twins, and not one among them has lost her young. ³Your lips are like a scarlet thread, and your mouth is lovely. Your temples are like a slice of a pomegranate behind your veil. ⁵Your two breasts are like two fawns, twins of a gazelle . . . ⁷and there is no blemish in you.**

Solomon is laying it on thick. There are numerous phrases in the *Song of Solomon* where you find typology. Sometimes, there is double typology. It is an extremely complex and wonderful book.

Look here where it talks about '**doves behind your veil.**' Remember, the doves are the eyes. It talks about in 1 Corinthians 13:12 how we see '**through a glass darkly.**' There is a veil, if you will, covering our eyes from heaven. You cannot look right up into the throne room of God. There is a veil there. Conversely, He certainly looks right through that veil and sees us intimately.

'**A flock of goats that have descended from Mt. Gilead.**' We stood at the base of Mount Gilead; which is actually a hill range, rather than a mountain. We watched as flocks of sheep and goats would come up over the top and run downward. It does remind you of hair. The same imagery is found in Isaiah 53:6 where it says '**all we like sheep have gone astray.**'

When it says '**flock of newly shorn ewes**' this is talking about her teeth. I had a dentist who came up to me and said, "Paul, did you notice that it says that not one of them is missing?" In other words, the Shulammite had all her teeth. We can find out quite a bit about her as we read the *Song of Solomon*. A flock of ewes also brings to mind the Lord Jesus Christ as a lamb that was led to slaughter, as it says in Isaiah 53:7.

'**A scarlet thread**' is talking about her lips. There is a scarlet thread between heaven and earth. Hebrews 9:22 '**without shedding of blood there is no forgiveness.**' There is a scarlet thread and it is Christ's blood, His atonement for you and for me.

**'Like a slice of a pomegranate behind your veil.'** Have you ever eaten a pomegranate? When you break it open, it has those thick kernels, all juicy and succulent. It is reminding Solomon of his wife's temples or her mind. He is there actually praising her mind, her thoughts, her temples. There was a veil covering the Holy of Holies in Jerusalem. Remember that the veil of the temple was rent from top to bottom as described in Matthew 27. We have access to God through the Lord Jesus Christ.

**'The tower of David . . . built with rows of stones.'** This citadel of David reminded Solomon of his wife's neck. It was all hung with shields that had metal bands. These were the shields of the mighty men. It would literally glisten in the sunlight. It is reminding him of his wife and her neck. She was wearing jewelry, a necklace. This tower was the morning newspaper. If the warriors had gone out during the night, the shields were taken off the tower. They were shields for battle. If you woke up in the morning and the shields were gone, this could affect your brother if he went out to war. It could affect your father, your husband, or your son. They needed to know if the shields were gone. But if the shields were hung around the tower, it meant it was a time of peace. The Lord Jesus Christ is called the Prince of Peace. If you want peace around your marriage, have Jesus, the Prince of Peace, near.

**'Like two fawns, twins of a gazelle.'** This is of course talking about her breasts. One of the sub-themes in the *Song of Solomon* is to always be positive. Never compare your spouse negatively to another person. Again here is the typology of Ephesians 5 where we are called the Bride of Christ.

> Always be positive. Never compare your spouse negatively to another person.

We see these verses and think, "How in the world are we ever going to use this 3,000 year old language?" Why don't we apply it. I asked this one man, "What do you like?" He said, "I like to fish." "Great, what do you fish for?" "Large mouth bass." "What is the biggest one you ever caught?" "Well, I caught a seven pounder." That's a good size bass and a good fight, I bet. I said, "All right, how would you describe your wife?" The guy did not even hesitate. He said, "She is a twelve pounder!" Some compliment! I asked another man, "So what do you like to do?" He said, "I like to bowl." "OK, what is your high game?" He said, "287." I said, "All right, how would you describe your wife?" "I guess she would be a 300, a perfect game," he answered. I asked another man, "What do you like?" He said, "Sports cars." "All right, how would you describe your wife, if you were going to build her up?" He said, "Oh, she would be a Lamborghini!" Wow, now that's a $250,000 boost to her self esteem.

In verse 7, when it says **'there is no blemish in you,'** does this mean this lady did not have a hang nail, did not have a mole? No. It meant he was **dwelling on his lover's good**. He was not looking at the blemish. He was not staring at the down side, the negative. He was finding the good.

"Praise for your bride is becoming." We have stood at the base of Mount Hermon, this massive three-peak mountain and on the high places of Mount Carmel, which is a whole range. Senir is at the southern end of the Carmel range. In these high places, the great golden eagle of Israel flies. No offense to America, but the golden eagle of Israel is far a superior bird to the American bald eagle. What a regal and majestic creature with a ten-foot wing span. It is massive. This golden eagle can look straight into the sun to spy out prey. It has a double set of eye lids, so it can pull down one lid to see its prey and still not have its eyes damaged. It can dive bomb at 200 miles per hour top speed, roaring down with those great talons onto its prey. Fabulous eyesight allows it to see miles to the most minute detail, 20:10 vision. Incredible.

But even more spectacular is the dignity of the mating process of the great golden eagle of Israel. When the female wants to find a mate, one that will really do the job, here is what she will do. She will fly down with her talons and pick up a branch. She will then take that branch up into the air about 1500 feet high and throw it out. The male will swoop down with all his power and try to catch that branch while it is in mid air. Then he will set it very carefully on the ground. If he passes that test, she will then take him to an even more difficult test. She will get an even larger branch and take this one up only about 1000 feet in the air and drop it. The male will dive with all his speed, trying to catch it. Now, what is she trying to do? She is trying to find a male that can build her nest and not drop it all over the ground and her eaglets with it. If he misses and drops that second branch, she is out of there and never has anything to do with him again. But if he catches it, she will then take him through the third, final and most difficult test. She will go down with her great talons and grasp a log, sometimes four inches in diameter, weighing many times her own weight.

The female eagle will take this up only about 500 feet, relatively close to the ground, and drop it, making it almost impossible for the male. But he will then streak with all his power and try to clasp that branch with his talons and set it very carefully on the ground.

If he passes that third and final test, this is what happens. The two of them will soar upward, straight into the sky, 10,000 feet high, two miles above the earth! There at that high place, they will face each other and come together with their talons and holding each other will free fall down through space, shrieking in delight. The eagles mate for life! Unlike the vulture that goes from mate to mate to mate. You will see a sick eagle and right by its side will be its mate. You will see a dying eagle and the last thing that dying eagle ever sees, right by its side, again will be its mate.

I was at a fast food restaurant early one morning. I noticed a couple that came in. They caught my eye because they were both wearing wedding rings. I would say he was in his mid nineties, and she was in her late eighties perhaps ninety. I watched as this couple ordered and got their breakfast. I waited as they sat down together, and the most amazing thing happened. His shaking hand, trembling and full of age spots, slid across the table. The most precious thing then occurred. Her hand slid into his hand and there in front of all of us, they bowed their heads and he quietly prayed for their breakfast. Commitment till the end.

The last picture I ever took of my parents was their hands holding each other, just before he died. After fifty-two years of marriage, the last snapshot was their hands. Your spouse's hand is more valuable than any amount of money, greater than any house, better than any job. When you hold that hand, it is the

> Your spouse's hand is the greatest treasure you will ever hold.

greatest treasure you will ever hold in your life. The *Song of Solomon* says, 'until the cool of the day, when the shadows flee away.' When is that? That is night time, when it's all said and done. You want to be holding that hand right to the end. God bless the hand that you married.

Song of Solomon 4:11, 12, 14-15, 'Your lips, my bride, drip honey; honey and milk are under your tongue . . . ¹²A garden locked is my sister, my bride, a rock garden locked, a spring sealed up. ¹⁴Nard and saffron, calamus and cinnamon, with all the trees of frankincense, myrrh and aloes, along with all the finest spices. ¹⁵You are a garden spring, a well of fresh water, and streams flowing from Lebanon.'

He is praising her here for so many things. In verse 11, he is praising her for her taste. He says, 'honey and milk are under your tongue.' The French did not invent this kiss. This is 1,000 BC! In verse 12, he is praising her for her fidelity. He says, 'a garden locked . . . a spring sealed.' She has been faithful. In verse 15, he is praising her for her walk with God. It says, 'a garden spring, a well of fresh water.' When you see words in here like 'myrrh,' 'cinnamon,' cassia, sweet 'calamus,' do you know what he is doing? He is speaking of the elements of the holy anointing oil of Exodus 30. It was literally the oil used to anoint the ark of the covenant and the tent of meeting. You talk about something honoring! He is using these elements to describe whom? His bride, his wife. **Praise for your bride is becoming**.

I have a really pretty bride. I noticed that when I was seventeen years old in math class. She was the new girl in school. I asked her out before anybody had a chance to. She said "No." The second time she said "No," too. Finally, as I was persistent, she ran out of excuses. Today, nearly thirty-five years later, she is a wonderful wife and mom. Her heart beat is so much for God in her children. I have watched as she has fasted for them, prayed for them, loved them and given to them. She has a lovely and beautiful soft voice. I just like to listen sometimes. It brings me peace. I can just hear the Lord through it. You know what I give her most honor for, though? She is a full of wisdom, the wisest person I have ever known.

> Praise for her is securing, not just to her but it's becoming to you as well

What about your bride, sir? Can you think of things that are praiseworthy about your bride? Dwell on them, praise for her is securing, not just to her but it's becoming to you as well.

Song of Solomon 5:1a, 'I have come into my garden, my sister, my bride; I have gathered my myrrh along with my balsam. I have eaten my honeycomb and my honey; I have drunk my wine and my milk.'

This is a man that is satisfied with his wife. He is praising her, thankful for her and reaching deep down to draw out the best about her. In his thought life, his emotions, his aspirations and general concepts about his wife. He's "gathered, eaten, drunk" things that are praiseworthy about his bride.

# 6 — Praise for Your Bride Is Becoming

# Chapter 7

# Fight for Love, Not Against It

## Fight for love, not against it.

I really enjoyed watching our son David crash through the line and make a tackle in high school football, or leg press 900 pound weights. In college I played enough collegiate football and was in the army for two years, that this fight thing is in me. There is a fight out there, but we need to not fight each other. Let's fight the battle **for** our marriages.

The power and authority to forgive are found in the person of Jesus Christ. Scripture is very clear about this. Matthew 9:6 and also Mark 2:10 say, **'the Son of Man has authority on earth to forgive sins.'** The Son of Man, that is the Lord Jesus. Now, if you are going to forgive, you need to start by opening up to each other. Your spouse is not going to find out by telepathy what you are upset about. You need to open up. So you are going to have to talk. It says in verse 6, **'I opened to my beloved.'**

Then, prepare for rejection. It says, **'my beloved had turned away and had gone.'** They are not usually going to get it the first round. "I can't stand the way you do that, it really bothers me." Your spouse does not usually say, "Oh, darling, I could not agree more. Aren't I awful?" That is not usually what is going to happen. They are usually going to come back with, "No, there's nothing wrong with what I'm doing." Start with being prepared to be rejected.

Then there is that effort and search for reconciliation. It says, **'my heart went out . . . I searched for him . . . I called him!'** Marriage takes effort! As a matter of fact, it takes a **lot** of effort, more effort than some people want to put into it.

I think we stop the Lord's Prayer too soon. We have a historical thing that we stop it at a certain spot. But are you aware that Jesus did not stop it where we stop it? He just kept right on speaking.

Matthew 6:13-15, **For Thine is the kingdom, and the power, and the glory, forever. Amen. ¹⁴For if you forgive men for their transgressions, your heavenly Father will also forgive you. ¹⁵But if you do not forgive men, then your Father will not forgive your transgressions.'**

Very strong words from Jesus Christ, wouldn't you say? Is forgiveness important? It is **critical** that we forgive and release each other in our marriages. Forgiveness actually is not optional to God; it is commanded.

## Steps of Forgiveness

Let's take some steps on the path of forgiveness. Step 1. **Know and RECEIVE the Forgiver**. You can know about God intellectually. Have you ever received Him as your own? To know and receive the Forgiver. He is the ultimate forgiver. He is the way in.

Step 2 is to **REQUEST a forgiving heart**. If you have asked the Lord to forgive you and you have received Him, now request a forgiving heart. You are not born with one. "God give me Your heart. Give me a soft heart. Give me a heart that is able to forgive my spouse and to live right in my marriage."

Step 3 is to **RELEASE your misunderstandings, hurts, pain** over to the Lord. The release of condemnation both for yourself in Christ and for your spouse.

Now you are ready for Step 4. Now **forgive your spouse**. Get the order right. We try to put Step 4 up at Step 1 and can't get through the thing. There is a reason. Forgive your spouse. If you forgive your spouse, it releases you as well.

---

## Steps of Forgiveness

**Receive** the Forgiver.
**Request** a forgiving heart.
**Release** misunderstandings, hurts, pain.
**Forgive** your spouse.

---

*Nasa* is the Hebrew for forgive. *Nasa* means to receive. *Nasa* means to respect. *Nasa* means to go on. Sometimes I think we need to go on, get past it. The same Hebrew word for "to forgive" also means "to marry!" Your marriage literally represents forgiveness! No wonder there is such a battle ground around marriage. Christ, when He speaks of Himself and the church in Ephesians 5, uses marriage to talk about the typology of Himself and His bride, the church.

## The Decision of Marriage

**Marriage is a decision, not an emotion**. "I'm falling in love," "I'm falling out of love." We hear this all the time. Sounds like you are mostly falling. Marriage is a decision. You have decided to be married. So guess what, you **are** married. It is not how you feel. As a matter of fact, when we wake up in the morning, sometimes we don't feel anything. We just want to get through the day. You may not "feel" married. But you **are**. It is a decision, not an emotion. To take the subjectiveness out of marriage and place it on an objective decision puts the couple on much firmer ground.

## In-Laws

The Bible is so wise. It knows us. It is **the** manual. It says, '**for this cause a man shall leave his father and mother and shall cleave to his wife,**' (Eph. 5:31). You would think it would say for this cause a woman should leave father and mother. We just did this. I walked my daughter down the aisle. She was so beautiful in her wedding dress that day, as I gave her away to this wonderful fellow. He really does love her very much. I, then, turned around and performed the ceremony. You would think it would say "For this cause a woman should leave father and mother." But it doesn't.

Think about this darling little baby — "Momma's little baby boy." Now he has grown up a little more. Now he's a toddler. Here he comes. Mom has him by the hands. "Momma's little baby boy." He grows up a little more. Now he is seven or eight years old. She is getting him ready to go out, combing his hair, brushing him off, straightening his shirt. "Momma's little baby boy." Now he is nineteen, twenty, twenty-one. He finds some nice young woman, and they get married. "Momma's little . . ." No. Right there is where it stops. Why? Because it says '**for this** cause a <u>man</u> shall leave his father and mother.' And cleave to whom? His wife. Leave and cleave.

## IT'S OUR HOME

In-laws can become outlaws, when we let them. There is a little phrase we like to use. "It's our home." Whose home is it? "It's our home." Suppose Mom and Dad come over to your house for dinner. Mom comes into the kitchen. She goes over, sees the canisters, straightens them up. Then she goes over to the refrigerator, opens the door, and makes a few comments. "Two percent milk would be better. You ought to have the meat down here and the vegetables up there." Then Dad walks into the kitchen and says, "Back in our home, dinner is always at 6:00. So tonight dinner's at 6:00." In your home dinner is always at 6:30. Remember whose house you are in. What time is dinner? Six-thirty, absolutely, very important. "It's our home."

The greatest relational tension statistically is between the man's mother and the man's wife. If that is the case with you, it means **you are normal**. If it is not so, don't worry about it. Whatever the issue, remember a little quick acrostic.

**H** usbands leave Father and Mother

**O** ur home

**M** others-in-laws and fathers-in-law lose, and in that win.

**E** nd the parental control.

Brothers and sisters can also become outlaws. We knew a family where the husband's brother knocked on their door and asked if he could spend the night there. They didn't have room for him, but he had brought his sleeping bag and offered to sleep in the kitchen. They agreed, so he spent that night, the next night and the next night. Three months later, the wife came to us and said "He's still in my kitchen!" We counseled them and said, "We think it's fine if he stays in your kitchen for another ten of even fifteen **minutes,** until he can roll up the bag and get out the door." So they told him. He rolled up the bag, got out the door, went over to the next town to another brother and pulled the same stunt with them. In-laws can become **outlaws** if we let them.

Our home is a place to **honor** Mother and Father. It says in Ephesians 6:1-3, '**Children obey your parents in the Lord.**' It tells all of us to honor our father and mother. They are two different Greek words in the original: obey and honor. Obey is for children. Honor is for all of us. Have your home be a place where Mom and Dad can be honored; have a wonderful dinner, at what time? 6:30. Brother can enjoy the stay all night long (one night). "It's our home!"

Be able to identify whether you are dealing with an **in-law** or dealing with an **outlaw.** Let's work our way through an acrostic IN-LAWS. In-laws will do the following things. You need to learn to identify if you are dealing with an in-law or an outlaw.

## *In-Laws*

An in-law will . . .

**Inspire by example**. We need to be an example to our married children. We should inspire them, but not force them or pressure them.

**Nudge them in the right direction**. Do not push, force, jam, or put pressure on them. But we do need to **nudge** them gently in the right direction.

**Love unconditionally**. An in-law will love them unconditionally. So often we will put conditions on our love. "As long as you have an exemplary marriage, as long as you take this job, then we will support your marriage." We need to be careful. We need to love them unconditionally.

**Allow them to make mistakes**. Did you ever make a mistake? We all make mistakes. We need to allow our married children to make mistakes.

**Wait for them to grow**. They are not going to have an instant, perfect marriage, are they? We need to allow them to make mistakes and wait for them to grow.

**Stand with them through troubles**. Every marriage is going to go through some troubles, some issues. We need to stand with them through those tough times.

**I** nspire by example

**N** udge in right direction

**L** ove unconditionally

**A** llow mistakes

**W** ait for them

**S** tand with them

## *Outlaws*

An outlaw will . . .

**Overstep their boundaries**. Do you remember the mother-in-law who came into the kitchen and was straightening up the canisters and the refrigerator? She was overstepping the boundaries of their home.

**Usurp the authority of the home**. Remember the father-in-law that came in and announced that dinner would be at 6:00? What was he doing? He was usurping that home, not honoring the identity the couple had formed in their home. An outlaw will usurp.

**Tough, too tough**. We can be too tough on marrieds. We need to be careful that we are not too tough on them, rather supporting and encouraging.

**Lean on them too heavily**. We knew a young couple. Their parents were **outlaws**. They came in and asked if they could borrow $1,000 right after the couple got married, which the couple gave them. The couple wanted to try to take care of their parents and honor them, but it was really hard. The parents no sooner took the $1,000 then they said, "That was good, but we want $2,000 more." This put real pressure on the young couple, married for about a month, who were wanting to care for their parents. Their parents really did not need the money, but were just coming into that young home and were being **outlaws**, demanding another $2,000. They came up with the money, but it was too expensive and it cost them their marriage.

**Aggravate**. When you have a sense of aggravation whenever your parents or parents-in-law come into your home, you may be dealing with an outlaw.

**Wrestle**. An outlaw will wrestle with them for authority over the children. We see this happen so often. The grandparents end up being outlaws. They come in and try to take the place of the parents in parenting the children. We need to be very careful not to wrestle for the affection of the grandchildren.

**Separate**. An outlaw will separate them, either by favoritism or by criticism. One is as bad as the other. Favoritism.

"Oh, my sweet Susie. She is going to get the most wonderful present for Christmas, and that thing she is married to is lucky if he gets a card." Do not separate them. Get them gifts that are for the two of them, which are going to build their home together. Do not separate them by favoritism or by criticism. "My sweet little Johnny, he is always doing the most for that hideous thing that he is married to." We end up criticizing them. It's a kind of unconscious thing we do, just a subtlety that can creep in and we end up separating them by criticism. You want to be building their marriage.

```
O VERSTEP BOUNDARIES
U SURP
T OUGH
L EAN TOO HEAVILY
A GGRAVATE
W RESTLE
S EPARATE
```

## Lions and Leopards

Marriage can have lions and leopards. There can be some very difficult or terrible things that can happen in the home. As a marriage counselor and as a conference speaker I hear so many stories, many things that are heart breaking. "Lions and leopards" hit the family. One couple saw their five year old little girl murdered. It happened right in front of the mother. Such a horrific thing. We knew another family that had a fourteen year old boy. The boy put a shotgun in his mouth and blew his brains out. Child suicide. You talk about something slamming a marriage. We knew a married couple where the wife had been raped while the husband was down at a work night at the church. This man knew her husband was going to be away. The rapist crawled in through a window. He did the whole thing in front of the kids. Many traumas you have to just give to God because of the blackness and the pain.

The next time life comes crashing and hits you, as it may, remember to be a servant lover. Life has difficult turns.

The world and life can come on a marriage like a lion. '𝔜𝔬𝔲𝔯 𝔞𝔡𝔳𝔢𝔯𝔰𝔞𝔯𝔶, 𝔱𝔥𝔢 𝔡𝔢𝔳𝔦𝔩, 𝔭𝔯𝔬𝔴𝔩𝔰 𝔞𝔟𝔬𝔲𝔱 𝔩𝔦𝔨𝔢 𝔞 𝔯𝔬𝔞𝔯𝔦𝔫𝔤 𝔩𝔦𝔬𝔫, 𝔰𝔢𝔢𝔨𝔦𝔫𝔤 𝔰𝔬𝔪𝔢𝔬𝔫𝔢 𝔱𝔬 𝔡𝔢𝔳𝔬𝔲𝔯'** (1 Peter 5:8). I was counseling a man who was on the verge of suicide due to marital pressures. After a number of sessions, I gave him this simple statement that he still credits with saving his life. I told him he needed to RAM the Lion. With Abraham of old, when he was on the edge of giving up his son, God provided a RAM. A RAM to blast the lion! RAM: **R**eject the negative, **A**ccept the positive and **M**ove into the challenges.

**R**eject the negative. Often in our homes and marriages, we need to mentally reject negative thoughts and pressures. "I can't make it." "This marriage will never happen." "We'll never be able to work it out or get along." The battle for the mind — RAM the Lion. Take the negative and reject it. "We're going to make it through this." "I *did* marry the right person." "We're going to hold on and better days are coming."

**A**ccept the positive. Finding the good, uplifting, positive is a real exercise. Look for it, grab hold of it and keep any positives near your heart, mind and thoughts.

**M**ove into the challenges. Marriage is a challenge, a big challenge. To consciously move into those challenges, with sexual issues, the kids, finances, jealousy, abandonment, whatever, isn't easy. To see them as something to overcome and conquer rather than to be defeated by can in itself give us the perspective we need. With heartbreaks (and marriage can have many) to RAM the Lion, hold onto what is dear in your relationship. Going through the difficult times together, waiting for the inner healing to manifest itself and allowing God to take you through are critical to any successful marriage. RAM the Lion.

When people say to you, "What is the big deal about your husband / wife?" what is the answer? **He is my husband! This is my wife!** That is what the big deal is. This is not your mate we are talking about. This is **mine**. When friends come around you and go, "Ah, he is just an idiot. Just drop him." Be careful. This is **your** marriage we are talking about here, not their marriage. Our daughter, Julianne, is a cheerleader. She's what they call "a flyer", the one they throw up in the air, while Mom and Dad are having heart failure. When she was little, her eyes just sparkled when she cheered at her junior high football games. Now she and her collegiate squad are competing for the national title at MGM in Orlando. I'm always hearing "GO, FIGHT, WIN!"

Here's a marriage cheer. "Forgiveness **Is** God's **H**ealing **T**ouch," FIGHT. So next time when you are in the middle of a FIGHT, recall Forgiveness Is God's Healing Touch. If it seems there is no way through this FIGHT, don't forget Forgiveness Is God's Healing Touch. The next time you are in the middle of a FIGHT, ponder Forgiveness Is God's Healing Touch.

> **F** orgiveness
> **I** s
> **G** od's
> **H** ealing
> **T** ouch

You have to be careful what you hear and what you believe from your friends. There was a man who was married and had a fine baby boy. His friends came around him and said, "You know, ever since you got married, you are not your happy, go lucky self." He said, "I'm not?" Did that thought ever cost him. He then began to go with them back to the bars and all the places they used to go, trying to be his "happy, go lucky self." Finally he was away from home so much that their marriage crumbled and fell apart. First one friend was transferred to another town. Another friend got a different job shift and could not go out with him any more. One friend after another left. Pretty soon he was all alone. Was he "happy, go lucky?" Not at all. He had no wife, no baby and, by the way, no friends.

One day Sandy and I were out for one of our 3 mile jogs. We do not break any land speed records, believe me, but, at least we will get out and get some fresh air. We were jogging along, finding a new dirt road, that we had never been up before, just trotting along, enjoying ourselves. Suddenly, up the road, here he came, **Mr. German Shepherd**. He was loose, and we were in his territory! Have you ever had these things that get stuck in your mind? All I saw was jaws and teeth, while this beast was making a bee line for us. I screamed, "It's a loose shepherd!" I sprinted in the other direction as fast as I could, and looked to my left, Sandy? No Sandy. Looked to my right, Sandy? Nope. She was back down the path right where we first saw the dog, standing there in the middle of the road with a big stick waiting for this animal! It was one of those moments. . . . Do I just leave her? I went back and tried to find some twig or anything to protect us. Standing beside her I said, "What are we doing?" She calmly answered, "Oh, we are going to stand him off." "Sandy, it's a shepherd." "No problem," she reassured me. I have never quite figured out what happened. I don't know if he looked into her big blue eyes and melted, as I have many times, or if she got a whack on the end of his nose. The dog stopped and took off yelping! We turned and began to jog, while I was looking over at Sandy with new respect. I don't think I have looked at her the same way since.

Marriage is similar. There are times when we need to stop and **fight for love**. If we had kept running, that shepherd would have gained on us. He would have had a hunk of fresh Paul leg meat. However, we stood together and fought for love. Whether its finances, in-laws, sexual temptations, job pressures, sickness, there are so many issues that can come in on our marriage. Through it all, **fight for love, not against it**.

*7 — Fight for Love, Not Against It*

# Chapter 8

# There Is Only ONE Unique Love in Your Life

There is a narcissistic, egocentric, pseudo psychology that is prevalent in our cultural environment now. The thinking goes something like this: One woman fulfills my emotional needs, another woman fulfills my sexual needs, and yet another woman fulfills my cooking needs. Contrary to this thinking is scripture. How many unique loves are there in your life? One!

There is only ONE unique love in your life.

## What Is Romance?

Song of Solomon 6:4-5, 9, 10, 'You are as beautiful as Tirzah, my darling, as lovely as Jerusalem, as awesome as an army with banners. 'Turn your eyes away from me, for they have confused me . . . 'But my dove, my perfect one, is unique . . . ¹⁰ "Who is this that grows like the dawn, as beautiful as the full moon, as pure as the sun, as awesome as an army with banners?"'

Solomon is laying it on here! What is romance? Noah Webster in his 1828 dictionary[6] (by the way, that was the best version) defined romance this way: "subjects interesting the sensibilities of the heart, the passions of wonder and curiosity, treats of great actions and extraordinary adventures, it vaults or soars beyond the limits of fact." He defines romantic as "wild, fanciful, extravagant in tastes, notions, expectations and zeal." Romance is four things. It's a decision, it's a climate, it's an atmosphere, and it's a feeling.

## ROMANCE IS A DECISION.

First of all, romance is a **decision**. It is deciding to be romantic. God placed the first couple in a romantic setting, Eden. Oh what a beautiful place! Think about Eden for a few minutes. Scripture says that four rivers ran out of Eden, so the Eden area was elevated, since water goes downhill. As you looked out you would be able to see a beautiful view from Eden. As a matter of fact, there was a mist that came up from the earth with natural shade, so you would be able to walk all day long and not get sunburned. Imagine the fragrance of the flowers that had just opened up for the first time. Feel the grass with your imagination, walking across meadows with that wonderful softness under your feet. No mosquitos, at least none that drew blood! What a lovely, romantic setting it was with the fingerprints of God, fresh across creation! Adam, Eve and God were all in the cool of the day together in Eden. So many people retreat by stating, "Well, I'm just not a romantic gal," or "I'm not a romantic kind of guy," but dwell on where God put the first couple. He put them in a romantic setting. Romance is first of all a decision, deciding to be romantic. We decide, "This needs to be part of our marriage, part of our relationship." Let's **decide to be romantic**.

## ROMANCE IS A CLIMATE.

Secondly, romance is a **climate** of how we treat each other, how we respond to each other. It includes the home duties that we are carrying for each other. It is the climate that we set. The climate can be warm and understanding for our love to grow, or it can be cold, frigid and stark — **we** make the climate.

## ROMANCE IS AN ATMOSPHERE.

Romance is third an **atmosphere**. It is an atmosphere of privacy, an atmosphere of nice clothing and pleasant fragrances, personal hygiene. *Song of Solomon* says, one who '𝔤𝔯𝔬𝔴𝔰 𝔩𝔦𝔨𝔢 𝔱𝔥𝔢 𝔡𝔞𝔴𝔫 . . .' 'an army with banners.' Solomon and the Shulammite are thinking about their first meeting. They are thinking about the first time they met when by his tents, those curtains were glistening and they had first found each other. To keep the romance alive, make it an **atmosphere**.

## ROMANCE IS A FEELING.

Fourth, it is a **feeling**. Allow yourself to be romanced and to reverse bad habits with that one unique love in your life. I hear this kind of statement all the time. "Well, I have been married so long. We have been married almost thirty years, now who needs marriage input?" The greatest increase of the divorce rate is in couples married thirty plus years. It is a full 10% increase right now. That is where the biggest jump, statistically, is. Why? We are dealing with the whole "empty nest syndrome." Careers are winding down, your children are getting grown, and suddenly you look at each other and see a stranger.

We knew this boy. He had a Sunday School teacher for years whom he had looked up to as his mentor. One day this teacher came into class and just announced, "Well, I have been married thirty years. I don't really see much point in going on with my wife anymore. We are just strangers. So I have decided to leave her." Saying that was easy for him, but for that boy he went home devastated.

> **Romance Is a**
> decision
> climate
> atmosphere
> feeling

Marriage and its romance do not need to end; it is meant to be a lifelong **adventure**. There was a couple at one of our conferences who had been married for sixty-seven years; I can still remember them. They came in with their walkers and made their way down to the front row. I was watching them taking all these notes, helping each other with their hearing aids. After the conference they came up to me and brightly said, "Dr. Freed, we learned a lot!" It surely is a life long adventure. It doesn't end.

Solomon calls her **'unique,' 'my perfect one.'** Now the Hebrew in the passage is sun. This is not the *shemesh* (orb), but it is the *chammâh* in the Hebrew, and that just means light and warmth. "You are my sunshine." We are talking about uniqueness. This means do not kiss another or hold another; don't be alone with another.

If you are in the ministry or a counselor, leave that door ajar or counsel with your wife or with another pastor in the room. Even if you are not stumbling, we have seen the counselee stumble. This can happen and literally ruin a person's effectiveness. We knew a pastor who had the woman he was counseling alone behind closed doors. Although he was unaffected, she got emotionally attached to him and became obsessed and fixated on him. She decided that they were really meant to be together. Finally, it drove him out of the pastorate. Be careful; I would encourage every counselor, particularly every minister, that you counsel with the door open or counsel with your wife or another man present.

## Romantic Investments

Let me give you ten romantic investments, ten things that can enhance your marriage.

### INVEST WITH YOUR CHILDREN.

**Number 1: Invest with the children with a view to strengthening your marriage.** If your marriage is just for the kids, it's not healthy. Sandy and I had a wonderful silver anniversary. Our kids sprung a whole surprise party for us. They got friends together and we had a tremendous celebration. They took us to the nicest restaurant in the city, had all these silver balloons and a fabulous dinner and even a silver wedding cake. They even gave us a cruise for our silver wedding anniversary gift. (Of course they hit up their grandparents for this.) It was wonderful. They had seen that our marriage was important, not just for us but for them too, and they are involved in strengthening our union. Invest with the children with a view to strengthening your marriage. Don't ever be ashamed to go out for dinner together and get a sitter for the kids. Invest in each other in your marriage and it will strengthen the whole family.

### INVEST WITH PRAYER.

**Number 2: Invest with prayer.** Have you ever prayed for your spouse? I'm not talking about praying with them. I'm saying just pray **for** them to be happy, unrelated to you. Pray that **they** will have a fulfilled life and that **their life** will be a joy. Take a moment and pray for your spouse, quietly in your heart, that God will bless them and they will be happy. Just pray a little prayer for them and pray for them often. "The one minute special." Invest with prayer.

*INVEST WITH TIME.*

**Number 3: Invest with your time.** You can have meat loaf, mashed potatoes, gravy and broccoli. The phone is ringing off the hook. Kids are screaming, TV's blaring. It's just "supper." But send the kids out for the evening. You say, "We can't afford a baby sitter . . ." Then find some other couple that is about your age and do a switch. We did this for years. We took their kids Tuesday night and Thursday night they took ours. It did not cost us for a baby sitter. So, send the kids out for the evening. Take the phone off the hook. (Who paid the phone bill? You did.) Turn the TV off; it will not break it. Turn the lights down, light a few candles, put on a little soft music. Now it's no longer meat loaf, mashed potatoes, gravy and broccoli. Now it's a **dynamic dinner**! The whole thing took a little bit of effort, a little bit of time. **Invest with your time** into your marriage.

*INVEST WITH FRIENDS.*

**Number 4: Invest with friends.** Have friends that she likes; have friends that he likes. Let it not be just friends that you want to be with, but friends that your spouse also enjoys. I would encourage you to get to know some other couples that are really building their marriage, which have some vision and want to go somewhere with their relationship. It is important that we have friends, friends whom we can share pain with, joy with, laugh and raise kids with, several couples with a common burden for successful marriages to be with. Invest with friends.

**Number 5: Invest in your faith.** So many churches have programs that are separating the family. We are getting programmed out. I knew a married couple with four kids that went to Sunday School every Sunday morning. He went off to a men's Sunday School class, while she went over to a women's Sunday School class. Find small groups where you can go **together**. Find activities and functions that will bring your marriage together. It is important that we invest with church life for married couples.

**Number 6: Invest with your finances.** Spend a little money on your marriage. You can have "weekend wonders," "adventure vacations." I had been planning for a year and a half to pull "an adventure" on Sandy. I diligently put away a dollar here, a dollar there. Sandy and I had planned to go out for an over night. We had packed for warm weather. She had her shorts and everything. As we were on our way downtown I said, "Look under your seat." She pulled out this package. "Wow, a present." I said, "Hurry up and open it up." She said "OK, OK," tore it open and said "Oh, my goodness, what's this?" Proudly I exclaimed, "Those are two tickets to Montreal, Canada. And we are late for the plane!" She said, "Paul, that's wonderful. But isn't it cold in Canada?" "Uh oh, I forgot." Eventually we made the plane, got her a sweater up there, and had a great time. However, if you try this one, remember to pack for the appropriate weather. Make your marriage an **adventure**. You want to make it sparkle. Invest with your finances.

*INVEST IN LAUGHTER.*

**Number 7: Invest in laughter.** Did you hear about the little boy that knocked at the bedroom door at the wrong time? You know what I mean by the wrong time, don't you? They said, "Go away. We're in here busy being married." He said, "Does that mean you are doing dishes or laundry in there?" Finally, they got him to leave and go back to bed. The husband turned to his wife and said, "You know, as a matter of fact, you are some dish. Now take off that laundry."

*INVEST WITH JOY.*

**Number 8: Invest with joy.** What gives you joy together? What is his favorite color? Do you know? What is her favorite dessert? With Sandy, it's those chocolate-covered caramels, but it has to be **milk** chocolate. I tried the dark chocolate before; it did not work at all. A singular, solitary flower. You can get a big bonus point for bringing home a single flower. You do not have to drop large money on the big bouquet. You can get just as much bang with a flower wrapped with greens and a ribbon. They are just looking for some consistency of your showing you are actually thinking about them. When you are going through the grocery store and you see those balloons, the ones that say, "I love you," spend the change and get a balloon.

How about giving a picture of a fun thing you did together? One day I slipped a picture out of the house when my wife was not looking. It was one with a flower in her hair. I got it enlarged to an 8 by 10 and framed it, wrapped it up, left it on the bathroom counter and went off to work. When I came home, it was up on the mantle. "Yes, a winner!" Find a picture, something that was fun: enlarge, frame and wrap it.

A newspaper interviewed me recently. They said, "Dr. Freed, bottom line what would you say a couple should do to strengthen their marriage?" I said, "**Have an affair**, with your spouse." Mercifully, they printed the whole line. Keep your marriage alive, make it exciting. Invest with joy.

### INVEST IN HER NEEDS.

**Number 9: Invest in her needs.** Remember the five greatest needs of a woman? They are affection, expression, communion, attraction and union. Let me simplify it a little. This is not really complicated.

## A woman's greatest needs:

**Affection**. Hold her. Hold her hand. Be affectionate to her without moving it toward a sexual advance.

**Expression**. Talk with her, not at her.

**Communication**. Give her your ear. Listen to her. Listen to everything she is saying. Let her share herself. Listen to her without snapping back answers

**Attraction**. Be attractive for her. It is not really complicated. Take a shower, put on nice clothes and cologne, and brush your teeth. It is really simple.

**Union**. Make love to her in a way that she enjoys.

INVEST IN HIS NEEDS.
**Number 10: Invest in his needs.**

**A man's five greatest needs**

These are the five greatest needs of a man.

## *Sexual Fulfillment*

Number 1. You guessed it. It is sexual fulfillment. A lady says, "Yep, that's probably number 2, number 3, number 4 and number 5 as well." No, ladies. It just seems that way. It's your fifth greatest need and his first greatest need. I want to spend a whole maxim on this one, so I'm going to wait until Maxim 10, a whole chapter on lovemaking.

Number 2, 3, 4 and 5 are to spend time with ERIC, E-R-I-C. Spend time with ERIC. I have all these little phrases, these things. Hopefully they stick in your head. People say these things stick in their heads for years. They can't get them out. Good. You want them to stick in your head. Spend time with ERIC.

## *Emotional Support*

E. Emotional support. Research has shown that it takes six to twelve non-sexual touches in any given day to maintain emotional stability in the marriage. Ladies, find his forearm. Put your hand on his forearm. Do three, soft, squishy squeezes. "I-love-you."

Again. "I-love-you." You have just knocked off half of his emotional needs for a whole day. These things work great. You get to a family reunion and turn around, "I-love-you." We need to be giving emotional support. I knew a man that came out of a near coma state after surgery. As his wife gave those three little squeezes, he responded back and came to.

## *Recreational Outlet*

R. Recreational outlet. You want to go fishing with him. Now, guys, don't get the biggest, juiciest worm you can possibly find and make her bait the hook with it. You want to go to a football game. I have been trying to get Sandy to go to a Bucs game for the longest time. I have a Bucs jersey. Alstott is my hero. He's a big fullback for the Tampa Bay Buccaneers. You'll forgive me. I don't know what your favorite team is. My son and I are always going to Bucs games when we don't have a conference. We try to get over there to take in a game. I've been trying to get Sandy to go to a Bucs game for the longest time. I traditionally would say, "Sandy, do you want to go to a Bucs game?" assuming she wouldn't want to go. Then one day she said, "Sure." I said, "What!" She said, "Sure, I'll go." I said, "You will?" She said, "I'd like to go." I was thinking, "Wow, this is going to be great!" We got some pretty good seats. It was a really close game. The Bucs were playing Minnesota. This guy behind us had this beer, pounding down beer number one, beer number two. I lost track at four. It got into the third quarter, and he was teetering around behind us there. He orders this huge beer. Alstott breaks loose, heads for the goal line, two guys hit him, he spins and scores. We all stand up and cheer. He goes, "Huahhh!" and his whole big beer goes right down my wife's hair, neck, back, dripping. I'll never forget the moment. She's standing there and looks over at me, "Paul, I have just fulfilled your recreational needs." Thank you, darling. I was so grateful that she at least came, at least showed interest. She really did come into my world. It was wonderful. Ladies, it can cost you sometimes. I understand that. You want to fulfill his recreational needs.

## Intellectual Stimulus

I. Intellectual stimulus. Believe it or not, ladies, there really is something between his ears. You want to go into his mind. Whether it is history, travel, books, research, business, computers (you at least want to know how to turn the thing on). You want to go into his world. You want to learn about his world. If he is reading a book, jump in and read it with him. Go into where his mind is. We have seen so many people separate on this issue. We knew this one couple where the guy loved history. His wife said "I want nothing to do with history." That little statement cost them their marriage. He took that personally, decided "She wants nothing to do with me." She wouldn't come into his world and be at all interested in history. Whatever the issue is, you want to go into his intellectual world.

## Companionship

C. Companionship. I'm going to tell on these guys. Ladies, these guys need you. They need you very, very badly. We have seen men make it through job loss, health loss, heart attacks, strokes because one particular person believed in them and stood by them. That person was their wife.

I had a chance to learn about this couple. Their names were Will and Cate Cohen. Actually, I interviewed their granddaughter. They had the second longest marriage in the history of this nation. They had been married for eighty years. The longest marriage is eighty-three years, during the Revolutionary War. I could not track that one back. But I got this one. Tell me everything, how they looked at each other, did they touch. She said, "As a matter of fact, she was always reaching over to Granddad and giving him these three little squeezes on the forearm. And he was always patting her on the cheek and telling her she was pretty and giving her these compliments. I said, "Did they have any advice for any young couples, you know, couples that had been married for only forty of fifty years?" She said, "Yeah, as a matter of fact, they did. They said this,

> **A Man's Greatest Needs**
> Sexual fulfilment
> Emotional support
> Recreational outlet
> Intellectual stimulus
> Companionship

'Work together through thick and thin. And most of all, trust God to guide you through everything you do." I said, "Whatever happened?" She said, "Granddad passed away." I said, "And Grandma?" She said, "Within about ninety days, Grandma passed away too." **'Until the cool of the day, when the shadows flee away.'** (4:6)

---

## Invest with

1 the children
2 prayer
3 your time
4 friends
5 your faith
6 your finances
7 your health
8 joy
9 her needs
10 his needs

---

# Chapter 9

# Let Your Marriage Be an Example

Solomon had exquisite gardens flowing over Jerusalem. Many are not aware of what he was doing with hydraulics, his water pools, fountains and piping systems. The Shulammite was walking through one of these lovely gardens as we read.

Song of Solomon 6:11-12, '**I went down to the orchard of nut trees to see the blossoms of the valley, to see whether the vine had budded or the pomegranates had bloomed. ¹²Before I was aware, my soul set me over the chariots of my noble people.'**

All of us are looking for answers, models and examples. The Shulammite was one day a fifteen year old shepherd girl, the next time she turned around, queen! That's a big leap. She had fallen in love and before she knew it — Israel's example. You get married, not thinking much of it, suddenly one friend breaks up, then another marriage breaks apart. Suddenly, people look at you and say, "Wow, you have a great marriage!" "You have been married for two weeks with no troubles." "You folks are still married!" Your marriage is an example and can quickly become looked at as a model.

The public is amazed at the most simple things. It has gotten so bad, just go in the grocery store and **don't fight**, be nice to each other, just be civil, and people will be amazed.

151

## Let your marriage be an example

It can shine. We have opportunities to have it glow like never before.

## Finances

The three greatest issues for marital break down are in-laws, finances and sex. Statistically, those are the big three. Let's look at finances and develop a priority list, ten priorities on finances. Finances are an issue in marriage and progressively an issue in this nation. Let's prioritize.

### HONOR GOD

Number 1: **Tithe and offering**. You want to honor the Lord first. Somebody might say, "I can't afford to tithe." You can't afford **not** to tithe. You really want God to bless your finances. You want to honor the Lord first. Haggai 2:8 'The silver and gold are mine.' They are God's in the first place. Bring the tithe into the church (the storehouse) (Malachi 3). Honor the Lord first.

### SHELTER

Number 2: **Shelter**. Get out of the cold, get out of the heat. You can live longer without food than you can without shelter. Stand outside when it's freezing cold and tell me whether you are thinking about a hamburger or getting on a sweater. We really need shelter.

### FOOD

Number 3: **Food**. This is not filet mignon and lobster. We are talking about the basics, meat and potatoes, vegetables, fruit, simple foods. We knew a couple who had a huge stack of restaurant receipts. They had thousands of dollars of receipts from the finest restaurants in town but had nothing else in life to show from eating out at these fabulous restaurants. Food essentials.

### UTILITIES

Number 4: **Utilities**. This is the home essentials, home repairs, a transportation vehicle, car repairs. You can get to work in a pickup truck. You do not have to have that fancy sportster. Many guys are amazed at this. Let's put major medical, catastrophic insurance, some kind of life insurance, at least some kind of term policy so that they cover your family, in this section.

### SPENDING MONEY

Number 5: **Individual spending money**. Every member of the family should have some financial expression. It does not matter who it is, everybody. A couple had their mom come live with them. They were receiving $1,000 a month from her Social Security check. She had to come to them and beg them, "Could I please, please have $10 so I could buy you a Christmas present?" That is wrong. Every member of the family, I don't care if it's a five year old little girl or whoever it is, needs to have financial expression. If your spouse has to borrow a dime to call home to see what you are watching on TV, something is amiss; spending money for all. We need to be sharing, everybody having financial expression.

## DEBT

Number 6: **Debt retirement**. Oh, is this an issue. We're talking about these little rectangular plastic things also known as credit cards. Has anybody had a credit card application come in the mail? You can get one a week. You can get one a day! It is getting so easy in the United States. In the United States and Western Europe, it is getting extremely easy to get way in over your head in debt. We knew a couple who had run up $50,000 in credit card consumer debt and were running $900 interest payments per month. It was eating them alive. One can really get strangled. If you are paying off the minimum balance only, guess who is winning the game? (Not you.) I want you to win it. Always pay more than the minimum balance, even if only a small amount, and move toward debt retirement.

## SAVINGS

Number 7: **Savings** for the emergency fund, some kind of savings put aside for special times and for special emergencies. If the refrigerator goes on the blink, we have some kind of savings set aside to do something about it, at least get it repaired. This is your reserve.

## JOY TIMES

Number 8: **Joy times**. This is for that special night out. Have some savings for that vacation, for that special time together. Whether you are coming up on your fifth anniversary or your twenty-fifth. What are you going to do? Plan for some special times, be saving out front so you can have a particular blessing together. It needs to be on the list, an investment in each other.

## INVESTMENTS

Number 9: **Investments**. There is an awful phrase that America cannot stand, "Slow, Steady Growth." Our culture detests that phrase. They want it now. They want it immediately. They want to get it bigger, better, instantly. What is our phrase? **Slow, steady growth**. It is going completely counter to what is happening in our society. It is a way to build your equity and to build your finances for the **long** term. I watched one family lose $18,000 in ten minutes, their entire life savings, when their stock option went the wrong direction. It was a "sure shot." It sure shot them. We must be careful. You are building with certificates of deposit, mutual funds, some solid blue chip stocks. **Slow, steady growth**.

## OVERFLOW BLESSINGS

Number 10: **Overflow blessings**. Here is where your boat is. Here is where the condo at the beach is. Here is where the sports car is. This is the big three-week cruise. It can be on the list.

There is no problem with it being on the list. But it needs to be number 10, not number 1.

## Financial Priorities

1  Honor God
2  Shelter
3  Food
4  Utilities
5  Spending Money
6  Debt
7  Savings
8  Joy Times
9  Investments
10  Overflow Blessings

# Ten Point Financial Counsel

### SAME TEAM

Number 1: **Be on each other's side**. Get on the same team. We see so many couples pulling against each other with their finances. You will get so much farther by being on the same side.

### BLESS YOUR SPOUSE

Number 2: **Do what is a blessing for your spouse**. We knew a man who liked jogging shoes; he collected about fifteen pairs. His wife had two pairs of shoes and asked him for a third. His response was that she would have to wait until after the latest model he wanted to get for himself came out. You want to do what is a blessing for your **spouse**.

### WITHIN BUDGET

Number 3: **Do not demand beyond your budget**. Have realistic budgets and work together to live within them. Don't pressure your spouse to push beyond your budget whether with credit card debt or extended debit. This only strangles your future.

### CAN THE MARRIAGE AFFORD IT

Number 4: **Do not pressure beyond what your marriage can afford**. Maybe your "budget" can afford it, but can the marriage afford it? This guy named Stew was married to Nancy. And Nancy had needs. She needed leopard skin outfits. She needed spiked gold shoes; she needed more and more jewelry. Stew worked a good job and worked hard at it. He worked between eight in the morning and six at night. One day he decided to take another job between 6:00 p.m. and 10:00 p.m.. I said, "Stew, why are you taking another job? Your job took care of all your family's necessities. What's the deal? Why are you taking this other job that is taking you away from your family?" Know what he said? "Nancy has needs." I said, "That is putting a lot of pressure on your marriage."

We were coming home late one night. Sandy, my wife, had been singing at a concert. We looked up at a scaffolding with spot lights on it. A man was hanging on the side of this house at 11:30 at night, scraping paint. I thought, "No, it couldn't be Stew, could it?" We stopped the car and I looked out and said, "Stew, is that you up there?" He said, "I've taken a third job between ten at night and one in the morning scraping houses." I said, "Why . . . ?" He said, "Nancy has needs." A true story! What was going on there? He was literally a slave to his love for her, and she was enslaving him.

Guess what happened. Late one of those nights, while he was out working, oppressed with eyes red and covered with paint scrapings, he found some other gal. Now Nancy has her "needs" and the three boys to raise by herself along with her gold spiked high heel shoes and no Stew. Do not pressure beyond what the marriage can afford even if you can squeeze it into the "budget."

### TIME BUYING CAUTION

Number 5: **The sorrow of time buying**. "All this furniture for only $239 a month for the next thirty years!" Long after the furniture is worn out, you have the $239 a month bill. There is a sorrow in time buying. When we "buy on time", we're actually selling our future. The joy is gone, the debt is present and the past gratification is long ago forgotten.

### ADVANCE FINANCIAL DECISIONS

Number 6: **Make financial decisions in advance**. Avoid impulsive buying. We live in an impulsive nation. Get it now, get it quickly, get it easy. Impulsiveness is pushing us all to a place where we don't want to go.

### BUYING CAPS

Number 7: **Put a cap on buying items**. You are going out to buy a TV and plan to spend $350. You get out there and the salesman says, "Oh, we have a special for today and just until 5:00 p.m.. You can have not only the TV but also this stereo unit and also the direct satellite link. You just need to sign right here. It is only going to be $779 and, of course, $89 for the hook up. Then it will be another $29 a month for the next fifteen years. Sign right here. This deal is good until 5:00 p.m." You went out to spend how much? $350. You did not go out to spend $779 plus the hook ups. Be careful with impulsive buying and put a cap on your purchases.

### COOPERATIVE BUYING DECISIONS

Number 8: **No major independent buying decisions**. We knew a couple that had an above ground pool. While the wife was off at work, the guy was at home and decided it would be a great idea to sell the pool. So, he sold the pool while she was away and decided to put a deck around the house. The wife came home from work, her pool had disappeared, and all these guys are crawling around her house building this deck. Did that put pressure on their relationship? Yes, really fast. What had he done? He had made several major **independent** buying and selling decisions. We're not talking about getting some chewing gum. We're saying no major independent buying decisions.

### COMPROMISE

Number 9: **Compromise**. Usually one of you is a little too frugal, keeping it back, a little too much of a tight wad. The other one is a little bit "Give it all away." Between the two of you there really is the balance for your finances. You want to be listening to each other. **Compromise**.

### RESPECT

Number 10: **Respect for your mate's place**. To respect your mate is really to honor yourself. We are the balance for each other if we will but listen.

---

## Financial Counsel

1 Same Team
2 Bless Your Spouse
3 Within Budget
4 Can the Marriage Afford It
5 Time Buying Caution
6 Advance Financial Decisions
7 Buying Caps
8 Cooperative Buying Decisions
9 Compromise
10 Respect

---

Joe and Sharon had been married thirty-four years. I inquired, "My, thirty-four years. Why so long?" They replied, "We hold hands, just like we did when we were first courting. We still hold hands wherever we go." These marrieds gave the whole credit for a thirty-four year wedlock to "holding hands." I think God means for our lives to be an example.

Shulam, where the Shulammite was from, was part of the tribe of Issachar historically. Issachar included the whole Nazareth region. This means the Shulammite was tending the flock and walking in the same places where a thousand years later our Lord Jesus Christ would walk. Walk where Jesus walks; in your marriage, follow Him. The world is screaming for examples. May God empower your marriage and my marriage to glow brightly in a dark and needy environment. The marriage that not only stays together, but reaches by its light to others, will be all the stronger.

# 9 — *Let Your Marriage Be an Example*

# Chapter 10

# Lovemaking Has Exquisite Delights

## Lovemaking has exquisite delights.

Solomon verbalizes his appreciation for her body and about his love for her as they are making love. Notice that his speech is always descriptive and gentle. It is never lewd and never coarse. He is honoring of her. He says, **'how beautiful and how delightful you are.'** He says of himself, **'the King is captivated by your tresses.'** He talks about her **'mouth like the best wine.'** He talks about her eyes as the **'pools in Heshbon.'** Heshbon was a Moabite city, very famous for its water pools and fertility. He does not isolate one part of her. He does not say, "I like your hair. And I also like your hair." He is going all over her body verbally. He talks about the curves of her thighs, her navel, her abdomen. Three times he mentions her breasts. He mentions her neck, eyes, nose, head, her flowing locks or tresses or braids, stature, breath and mouth. Notice what is happening; gentle stimulating foreplay is here in verse 8 as he says, **'I will climb.'** He is moving with passion in verse 8 talking about **'taking hold of her.'** You can hear him saying, **'Oh.'** He refers to her **'mouth,'** as they are continuing to **mouth kiss** in their **lovemaking**. I like to call it lovemaking, not sex, because it comes out of a whole life together. It does not start in the bedroom.

Sex therapists and psychologists are beginning to come back to what I would consider are **biblical norms**. They are saying things like, "Kiss more on the mouth; it enhances lovemaking." All one has to do is read the *Song of Solomon*; they are mouth kissing throughout the book. Counselors are saying, "Seek seclusion." So much for the public sex. They are saying, "Privacy actually enhances lovemaking." "Change scenery" is another suggestion. Well, why not just read *Song of Solomon* with multiple scenes and much lovemaking. They are advising "greater dialog and communication" to help lovemaking. Again you could not get better dialog and communication than is in the *Song of Solomon*. They are open and warm to each other, what a model!

### *Music*

Music enhances lovemaking. Research shows that music triggers emotional responses and improves lovemaking. The brain stores up pleasurable memories. When the memory is associated with music and you hear it, the pleasant memory is replayed. One hears that phrase, "They are playing our song." There really is something to that. It is called the *"Song" of Solomon*. The whole book is a song. Music is meant to be a very important part of our relationship with each other.

### *Total Intercourse*

When the King mentions, 'your mouth is like the best wine,' (Song of Solomon 7:9a) she finishes the sentence for him, 'it goes down smoothly for my beloved' (Song of Solomon 7:9b). So their intercourse is **total**. It is sexual, it is emotional, it is psychological, and I might add it is also **spiritual**. They are in a sense worshiping God by their marriage and by their lovemaking together. Their intercourse is total.

Song of Solomon 7:10, **I am my beloved's, and his desire is for me.**

We have been following this as one of our many sub-themes. The two major themes in the *Song of Solomon* are the purity of marital love and the power of marital love[7]. In 2:16, she says, '**my beloved is mine and I am his,**' with the orientation on herself. As she matures, she says, '**I am my beloved's and my beloved is mine**' (6:3). She has reversed the order. But look what has happened by the time you get to 7:10. All the orientation for this woman is off herself and onto to her husband. '**I am my beloved's and his desire is for me.**' Now this did not just happen. This is a woman who has been **fought for, not against**, whose **good has been dwelt on**, who has been received in her **womanhood**. All these kinds of actions by her husband have been affecting her. Now she is able to give herself more fully and completely to him.

Song of Solomon 7:11, 12; 8:3, '**Come, my beloved, let us go out into the country, let us spend the night . . . ¹²There I will give you my love. 8:3 Let his left hand be under my head, and his right hand embrace me.**'

It is the woman that is doing the initiation of the romantic places where they will go and share their love with each other. It's coming from **her**. She says in verse 12, '**there I will give you my love.**' She is making promises she is going to keep! In verse 13 it talks about, '**choice fruits, both new and old.**' So variety and excitement are important in lovemaking. It's not the rote of "Monday and Friday, 8:05 in the evening, right-hand side of the bed, 45° angle, ready, go", not at all. It is meant to be **excitement and joy**.

The scripture speaks of '**the mandrakes**' and '**pomegranates.**' Those were considered the aphrodisiacs of the day. They taste sweet and wild at the same time. What are our pomegranates and mandrakes now? Romantic dinners, candle light, music, flowers, cologne and perfume.

The Janus Report[8], a fascinating study of sexuality in the United States, came out with some really interesting statistics; 74% of all women over the age of 65 engage in regular, weekly sexual activity. So there is hope, guys! Lovemaking does not go away. I asked this couple who had been married 61 years. "Do you still have fun? Do you still kiss?" She exclaimed, "Oh, yes, do we still kiss? Big ones!" It is meant to be a lifelong enjoyment.

## *Lovemaking Troubleshooting Twelve*

**Number 1: Do what is sexually enjoyable for your mate.** Did I say what is sexually enjoyable for you? No. I'm writing to both of you.

**Number 2: Avoid things physically hurtful in sexual activity.** Lovemaking is meant to be delightful. It is not meant to be painful; it is not meant to be hurtful.

**Number 3: Don't pressure your mate for sexual times or positions.** It's not "only at midnight, swinging from the chandelier, upside down." Skip the pressure, enjoy the relationship.

**Number 4: Wives be sensitive to your husband's need for greater frequency of lovemaking.** Although this is a sensitive issue, it would help if couples would just remember this little phrase, "Men need more times, women need more time."

For men, although quality, passion and sensuality are important, all that pales behind straight quantity. To make love often is extremely important to a man. His needs build and, as one man recently put it to me, sex solves all problems: headaches, sleeplessness, nervousness, back aches etc. Although that may be exaggerating the effectiveness of sexual frequency, it certainly points to a key issue. "Be sensitive to your husband's need for frequency."

***Number 5: Avoid using the need to be pregnant for lovemaking, rather than care for each other.*** We arrived at this point from working with so many couples dealing with infertility. Children should come out of your lovemaking time. Motivationally, do not make love to have children. Get the order right from the very start of conception. The motivation is your marriage. If you are staying together for the kids, you are staying together for the wrong reasons. Stay together for **each other**. Let the children receive the joy coming out of your union and the security from your marriage. If you are unable to have children, then there is the whole adoption option. However, when you make love, keep your own relationship primary.

***Number 6: Encourage each other sexually.*** Never compare your spouse to somebody else. I knew a woman who told her husband, "Of all the guys I ever had, you are the best." Stupid lady. That was the wrong thing to say. Do not compare your spouse with someone else. To build each other up with approbation, encouragement and compliments can only enhance your enjoyment of your sexual times.

**Number 7: Release each other from sexual mistakes of the past.** This could be mistakes you have made with someone else. It could also be when you have not been sensitive in your own marriage, when you were callous and were not careful with each other. Release each other from sexual mistakes of the past. The pounder of the past will try to haunt the joys of today and tomorrow. Go on, move ahead and release yesterday's mistakes to the fulfilment of the future.

**Number 8: Build your knowledge of lovemaking from godly sources.** Don't get your knowledge from pornography or cheap romance novels. It is just going to delay your satisfaction that God means for you to have with each other in your marriage. We need to get fulfilment and joy right here in this union, not looking outside it for fulfilment. Why go into a fantasy world of emptiness and loneliness when we can have the power and joy of each other's marital passion.

**Number 9: Have realistic expectations for each lovemaking time.** If it needs to be "quick," if you are tired, if there has been sickness, a death in the family or some issue, take it easy on each other. Lower your expectations. If you are rested, you have a romantic setting, you can get away for a while with each other, then raise your expectations a **little**. Be careful not to put pressure on your marriage, "It has to happen tonight. If it's not explosive this weekend, I know we are not going to make it." Do **not** do that to each other. Marriage functions best when it is not boxed in, pressured, with unrealistic expectations put over it. It is a **life long adventure** we are on together. You are building for the future. Have realistic expectations for each lovemaking time.

**Number 10: Privacy in intimacy is essential.** Get a lock for your bedroom door. If you can't afford a lock, then push the dresser up against the door! But get **privacy**. We knew a couple who had a two year old and a four year old. Whenever they went to make love, they threw the kids in bed with them so they would know just where they were and proceeded. That was not good for the kids and not good for their marriage. Privacy, please.

It goes beyond that. We are also talking about **verbal privacy**. Do not bring Mommy and Daddy into your bedroom! It is not a kiss and tell event. By the way, your hairdresser and buddies at the gym are probably not the world's greatest sex therapists. Privacy and intimacy are two joys of marriage. Both build on mutual trust and respect.

**Number 11: Avoid too much time going by without making love.** If your schedule is too busy to make love, your schedule is too busy! We need to avoid too much time going by without making love. People are always interested in the national average. I often tell people it really doesn't matter because those stats just pressure us wrongly. The national average is 2.7 times a week. Somebody asks, "How do you get the point 7?" I guess they were interrupted! It does not matter if you are having sexual union more or less than that. What matters is that you are avoiding too much time going by without making love.

**Number 12: Remember the importance of gentleness in lovemaking.** It is not rough, tough, gruff sex. It is the **gentle, joyful fulfilment** of your lovemaking together. Foreplay, tenderness, understanding and sensitive care for your spouse will lend itself to fulfillment and peace in your time together.

If we can remember a couple of words, it will help. Guys, your words are **Protection** and **Affection**. Ladies, your words are **Excitement** and **Fulfilment**. Lovemaking does indeed have awesome potential in marriage, and these simple guidelines will take you miles down the journey to these exquisite delights.

## Lovemaking Troubleshooting Twelve

1  Do what is sexually enjoyable for your mate
2  Avoid things physically hurtful
3  Don't pressure your mate
4  Be sensitive to your husband's needs
5  Avoid using the need to be pregnant
6  Encourage each other sexually
7  Release each other from mistakes of the past
8  Build your knowledge from godly sources
9  Have realistic expectations for each time
10  Privacy in intimacy is essential
11  Avoid too much time going by
12.  Remember the importance of gentleness

## 10 — Lovemaking Has Exquisite Delights

# Chapter 11

# Faithfulness
# Brings Peace

Do you want trouble, heartache and pain? Then bring somebody else into your marriage bed. Everything changes instantly. Bring in another woman, bring another man into your marriage, and things turn upside down. Unfaithfulness and its agony can last for months or even years.

## Faithfulness brings peace.

The opposite is, unfaithfulness brings heartache, war, turmoil and agony of heart and soul.

Song of Solomon 8:5a, **'Who is this coming up from the wilderness, leaning on her beloved?'**

Adam and Eve had sinned and were put out of the Garden. They were put out of Eden, into the **wilderness**. But look what is happening here. The couple is coming up out of the wilderness, moving toward the narrator, God. They are traveling leaning on each other, coming toward God. It is a beautiful picture of the restoration of the marital relationship coming out the wilderness of sin. It comes out of the pain and agony of the loneliness of deprivation outside Christ and toward the Lord Himself.

Song of Solomon 8:6-7, **'Put me like a seal over your heart, like a seal on your arm. For love is as strong as death, jealousy is as severe as Sheol; its flashes are flashes of fire, the very flame of the LORD. ⁷Many waters cannot quench love, nor will rivers overflow it; if a man were to give all the riches of his house for love, it would be utterly despised.'**

These are strong words. Put your hand over your heart. Almost everyone puts it on the left side; that is correct biologically. That is where the largest portion of the heart is; the strongest heart beat goes to the left. The Hebrews felt the arm included from the fingertips to the shoulder. The Romans picked up on this, and the left arm is where the seal was placed, representing the seal on the heart. This was the wedding ring. It says **'seal over your heart, seal on your arm'** (Song of Solomon 8:6). That is how the wedding ring got on the left hand, symbolizing the heart. We fly all over the country, and it is so difficult to see when men take off their wedding ring and put it in their pocket. As they take off their wedding ring to flirt with the flight attendants or some other passenger, it is accurate. It isn't sealed in the heart and so it comes off the hand. The adulterous eyes start looking around; the adulterous heart is wandering. Set a seal on your arm, a seal on your heart.

If it is a choice between your job and your marriage, there is no

> Choose your marriage.

choice. Chose your marriage. If it is a choice to have a bigger house and it is going to cost you your marriage, there is no choice. **'It would be utterly despised.'** If it is a choice between your kids and your marriage, choose your marriage. If the choice is between your in-laws and your marriage, choose your marriage.

## Wall or Door

Song of Solomon 8:8, 9, **'We have a little sister ... 'If she is a wall, we shall build on her a battlement of silver; but if she is a door, we shall barricade her with planks of cedar.'**

I received a phone call several years ago from a pastor. He said, "Dr. Freed, we have a little problem in our church. We wonder if you wouldn't mind coming over here and doing a marriage conference." I said, "I would be happy to, but what is the 'little' problem?" "Oh, no big deal, just a little problem. It has come to my attention in the last week that seven different members of our choir are simultaneously in adulterous relationships with other members of the choir. And they all want to continue

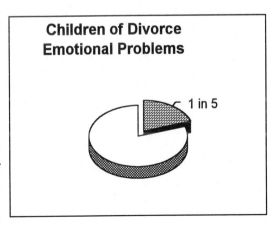

**Children of Divorce Emotional Problems**

1 in 5

to stand up on Sunday, wear their robes and sing." I said, "Sir, you do not have a **little** problem." If this is what is going on in the choir, and this is what he found out in the last week, then what is going on in the whole congregation? The church, if she is a 'wall,' in other words faithful, 'we will build on her battlements of silver;' we will encourage her. But if she is loose, if she is a 'door,' 'we will barricade her with planks of cedar.' We have a responsibility to encourage her fidelity.

## Children of Divorce

People say, "Well, I don't know. If it's good for the adults, it's good for kids. Whatever the adults want to do is OK. Let the kids find their way." This is just not true. It does

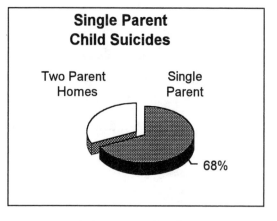

affect the kids. As a matter of fact, one in five emotional problems in children is going to come out where the parents are separated or divorced.

How about this for an unbelievable statistic: 68% of all child suicides happen in a single parent home? Sixty-three percent of all children born after 1987 will have lived

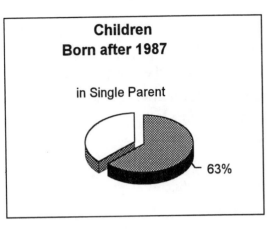

**Children
Born after 1987**

in Single Parent

63%

part of their childhood in a single parent home, most kids! You talk about future shock. It's coming! Each year spent in a single parent family will reduce a preschooler's educational attainment by one fourth of a year. In other words if a child spends eight years in a single parent home, he or she will be two full grade levels below their peers on average. It **absolutely** affects the kids.

Our children are the **fruit**, not the root. **Fruit not root**. They are not the foundation of your marriage. They are the fruit of your marriage.

So what was the Shulammite? Was she a door or was she a wall?

Song of Solomon 8:10, '**I was a wall, and my breasts were like towers; then I became in his eyes as one who finds peace.**'

The Shulammite was a wall. As a matter of fact, she says her **'breasts were like towers.'** She is really plain about this. Her fidelity brought him **'peace,'** and it certainly goes both ways.

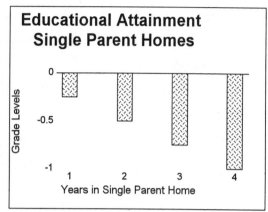

**Educational Attainment
Single Parent Homes**

Grade Levels

Years in Single Parent Home

## Adultery

Let's look at adultery. If you are the adulterer,

**1. Own it.** Just own it. None of these excuses, "Ah, if my wife had been a little more understanding of my needs." "If my husband had been a little more sensitive to me, I would not have found myself with that other guy." Just say this is **my** error. Own it.

**2. Be aware of the difference between forgiveness and restoration**. How long does forgiveness take? It is instant at Calvary. That is the power of the Cross. There is instant forgiveness. But restoration can take weeks, months, years, maybe a lifetime, but certainly worth all the time, effort, love and understanding it will take.

**3. 75% of all marriages of individuals who marry their adultery partner end in divorce.** It is the highest statistic of all. It does not work. It is the wrong foundation to build a marriage on. A marriage that is built on deception, unfaithfulness and theft is doomed to repeat failure.

**4. Rebuild.** Then look to rebuild that marriage, to rebuild your children, to rebuild everything around you. Maybe you cannot put the marriage back together, but you can speak for marital fidelity and purity. You can do everything in your power to promote marital faithfulness. By the way, distance emotionally and physically, if possible, from your adulterous partner is critical.

> Distance emotionally and physically, if possible, from your adulterous partner is critical.

If you are the one that adultery has been committed against, you really have only two options. You can either take the Matthew 19:9 "exit clause" where it says, 'except for immorality.' This was Christ speaking. One can say, "This has broken the covenant, I cannot go on. This adultery has ended the marriage. I am done." That is one option. Or you can take another option where you state, "I want to rebuild. I want to go on. I want to forgive from the bottom of my heart, and I want this marriage to be restored."

I had the privilege to perform a remarriage of a couple that had been married and then divorced for ten years. Later, I was on a live radio program and a young caller dialed in. It was their son on the air to thank me for bringing his parents back together. He wanted to tell me live on the radio that he was now getting married. He shared that he really had his hopes and dreams of marriage restored by the fact that his parents got back together.

So often though, couples take neither option but do something halfway between. They do what is called a "trial marriage." What is a "trial marriage?" That is an oxymoron. We end up repeating and reminding our spouse of the error. This undercuts the ability to rebuild the marriage at all. I say get out or get in! And if you are getting in, do it with all your heart. Although it will take everything the couple has to make it happen, it's worth it.

Have you ever thanked your spouse for being faithful? Or have you just assumed on each other? So many people think, "They better be faithful." But, it's not that way. It's not by compulsion. It is by our free will. Thank your mate gratefully for their faithfulness. Perhaps there has been unfaithfulness. Then, have you even thanked them for their recent faithfulness? Graciousness and gratitude are wonderful nutrients for a fruitful marriage.

Be faithful in your marriage, and you will have peace.

# Chapter 12

# Friends Are Good, But Remember Your Beloved

# Friends are good, but remember your beloved.

There is a term that has now reached into our common language, and that term is "empty nest."[9] For couples whose children have reached that milestone of now being off to college, jobs, marriages of their own, this is your opportunity.

I would greatly encourage younger couples or couples with shorter marriages (under five years) to build these principles into your marriage early. For couples that are now experiencing empty nest issues, here are a few must do's.

1.  Have friends that share your principles, entertainment and life together. Get a couple of couples whose anniversaries, kids' birthdays you both know, whose fun spots you share and whose company leaves you warm and closer together as a couple.

2.  Pursue hobbies, interests, music, travel together. Move into the adventure of going places and getting out together.

3.  Have a new project together. Get going on writing, collecting, visiting, whatever. But do it together.

4. Have a ministry, charity or church activity that you do together.

5. Mentor. Have another younger couple or younger people that you are advising, leading, helping and nurturing. How fulfilling to have your knowledge and understanding passed on to others.

So when you have friends beside you, interests and projects around you, God above you and the young receiving from you, you're covered. The nest is packed and your lives count for so much more than you ever thought they would.

There are many things that can call themselves our "friends" and many things wanting to be part of our marriages. Many things vie for our attention.

Song of Solomon 8:13, '**O you who sit in the gardens, my companions are listening for your voice — let me hear it!**'

This is the last time in the *Song of Solomon* the King speaks.

Can you hear the heart of God in that? '**My companions,**' **the world**, are listening, Church, for your voice. "**Let me hear it.**" Get the good news out there. The world needs it. '**My**

**companions are listening for your voice'**, Church. Speak it to them.

## Marriage Breakers

Here are five marriage breakers. We want to be **Marriage Makers**, not marriage breakers.

### *Marriage Breaker #1*
#### *Broken Home Repeater*

**Broken home repeater.** This means either you or your spouse have come out of a broken home, that your parents were divorced or separated. There gets to be a repetition of the broken model. This subtly lands in your head and gets imprinted in there. It is the model that keeps getting repeated generation after generation. We need to break it and be non-repeaters and be Marriage Makers.

I talked to a gentleman in Savannah, GA, who told me of his grandparents who were married for more than fifty years. They had six kids. All of them got married and stayed married all their lives. They had twelve grandchildren, all of them married and were still married. They have, so far, eighteen great-grandchildren. Now what are the chances for those great-grandchildren staying married? They are pretty good. It is their whole model proceeding generation after generation. If you are a "first generation Marriage Maker," that is a great place to start.

Make this union last. We need to take this on for our children and our kids' kids. We need to be looking to be **non-repeaters** when it comes to marriage breakers.

## Marriage Breaker #2

### *Parental Rejects*

**Parental rejects.** Maybe your parents have rejected you. There are so many reasons why you can be rejected. You can be rejected for doing the wrong thing, maybe rejected just because you were born and put up for adoption or abandoned. You can be rejected by your parents for doing the right thing. "Holier than thou, you think you are too good for us, don't you?" And you are just trying to live right. The key is if you have been rejected by your mother, rejected by your father, to come under the **acceptance** of your Father in heaven. He loves you and **you** especially. He cares about you and you specifically. You are **His** son. You are **His** daughter. Come into the acceptance of your heavenly Father.

## Marriage Breaker #3

### *Abuse*

**Abused.** Does this open up a can of worms! Molestation, incest, rape, alcoholism, violence, are all forms of abuse that have so much pain associated with them. We knew a woman who had been raped. It was very sad. My wife and I counseled with her, and she was really wrestling with the whole thing. We said to her, "You really need to release your rapist to God. You cannot hold that bitterness and anger. It will just eat you up." We watched as she struggled. Suddenly in the middle of the counseling session, she hardened. I watched it happen as she said, "But I hate him. I will always hate him." You know what she did? She followed him throughout his trial. She was right there in the front row, gritting her teeth at him. When he was incarcerated (they sent him to five years of federal penitentiary, his second offense), she was there on incarceration day, making sure he was locked up. He is now out of prison, but she is still in jail, the prison of her own bitterness, hatred and anger.

The answer is to get out there and be used for the glory of God. If you have been abused, have been through a tough time, get out there and let the Lord use your life for something. Let him use it for His glory, use it for the kingdom of Heaven. Take your eyes off yourself and put them on Him. Get busy for the things that are good and right and useful. Fill your life and heart with usefulness, and leave the pain behind.

## Marriage Breaker #4

### Troubled Teens

**Troubled teens.** If you have a normal teenager (what is a normal teenager?), I have four words of hope for you: "This too shall pass." They can't stay teenagers their whole life. They eventually have to hit twenty, at least in numbers. However, here I am writing about the deeply troubled teen, a teen where there is violence involved or drugs. They can be marriage breakers if we let them. If you have a troubled teen, you want to pick the battles you can win! You do not have to fight every battle, just because **they** want to fight it. You can just skip that particular fight. But you do want to give two messages to your teen. The first message is, "I love you. You are mine. You will always be my son, always my daughter, always be dear to my heart." You have to get that message really plainly to them. The other message is not very complicated. It is, "No." Just two letters, No. "No, you cannot bring drugs into our home. No pornography at our house. No." You have to give both messages. If you just give one, they take it as rejection. If you give the other by itself, they take it as license.

General George Patton was great at fighting the right battles. He was a World War II general that just wanted to get to that goal, Hitler in Berlin, and saw it clearly in front of him and went for it. Pick your battles wisely and win.

Teen Tamers is what we want to be. Remember, finally, leave them with God.

## Marriage Breaker #5

### *For Better*

**For better** is a marriage breaker. We say, "for better or for worse." We are realistically thinking for better and for **better**. We are not thinking for worse. No one gets married for worse. We have to be careful because this can be a marriage breaker. We need to be "For Worsers." So often marriage can end up being difficult, marriage is full of "for worse" situations. God means for us to be "For Worsers."

I will never forget this one couple that came up to us at the conclusion of a conference. He was shaking, kind of trembling and seemed extremely weak. His wife had her hand under his elbow, steadying him. They explained that two years ago he had gotten terminal cancer. Timidly, he said, "The last ten days I have been in the hospital. Literally the doctors felt like this was the end and I would never come back out. I really went to the hospital to die. But we heard about your conference and I got special permission from my doctor to get up out of my death bed and come. The last thing we wanted to do together was to rededicate our marriage to each other and to the Lord." I looked over into her eyes; I thought I was looking into heaven. They were crystal clear. She was looking at me gently saying, "That's right. That's right." I was looking right into the eyes of a "For Worser."

---

## Marriage Breakers

Broken Home Repeater
Parental Rejects
Abuse
Troubled Teens
"For Better" Not Worse

---

## Conclusion

So, whatever happened to Solomon and his wife the Shulammite? Where did these thousand wives come in? Here is what I believe happened. There is an obscure scripture in 1 Kings 4. It speaks of the political cabinet of Solomon and mentions a number of his ministers and a number of his children. There are two baby girls spoken of here. The first girl's name is *Basmath*. *Basmath* means balsam. It's a spice. This is one of the only places in scripture where a spice is the proper name of a person. The second girl's name is *Taphoth*. *Taphoth* means myrrh (the burial spice). *Song of Solomon* chapter 5 verse 1, **'I have come into my garden, my sister, my bride'** (in other words, they have made love), **'I have gathered my myrrh along with my balsam!'**

I believe the *Song of Solomon* was written as a eulogy to his young Shulammite bride that had just died giving birth to their second baby girl, and he has named her Myrrh, the burial ointment. There he is holding Myrrh, with Balsam, his other little girl, right by his side. The rest of his life was he trying to fill some huge void in his heart? It says **'chosen of a thousand'** (5:10). Was he trying by these seven hundred wives and three hundred concubines to fill this void left by the Shulammite? We will never really know until we get to heaven.

This is what we do know. We do know the Bible opens with a marriage, Adam and Eve. It starts right in the beginning of the book. There is also a marriage there in the center of our Bible, the spousal love of Solomon and his bride the Shulammite. Finally the Bible closes with a marriage, the great marriage supper of the Lamb! The last book of the Bible, the last chapter of the last book of the Bible says these words, **'And the Spirit and the bride say, "Come" . . . Even so, Come, Lord Jesus.'**

Marriage, God's height, God's best has been given to us as a gift from His very throne. As the most embattled institution of our day, may every married fight for its dignity, explore its wonders, work for its fulfilment, and in a society that so needs us be. . .

## The Marriage Makers

*The Marriage Makers*

# Endnotes

1. Whitehead, B. D. *The Divorce Culture*, Knopf, 1997.

2. John Foxe, *Foxe's Book of Martyrs*, 1556.

3. "Should This Marriage Be Saved," *Time* February 27, 1995.

4. Schwambach, S. *Tough Talk*, Harvest House Publishers, 1990.

5. Waite, L. *Natural Health*, December 1995.

6. Noah Webster, *American Dictionary of the English Language*, Converse, 1828.

7. Glickman, S. C. *A Song for Lovers*, InterVarsity Press, 1976.

8. Janus, S. S., and Janus, C. L. *The Janus Report on Sexual Behavior* John Wiley & Sons, 1994.

9. Dobson, J. *Focus on the Family*